The
Big
Peace

The Big Peace

Find Yourself Without Going Anywhere

Suzy Greaves

HAY HOUSE

Australia • Canada • Hong Kong • India
South Africa • United Kingdom • United States

First published and distributed in the United Kingdom by:
Hay House UK Ltd, 292B Kensal Rd, London W10 5BE. Tel.: (44) 20 8962 1230;
Fax: (44) 20 8962 1239. www.hayhouse.co.uk

Published and distributed in the United States of America by:
Hay House, Inc., PO Box 5100, Carlsbad, CA 92018-5100. Tel.: (1) 760 431 7695
or (800) 654 5126; Fax: (1) 760 431 6948 or (800) 650 5115. www.hayhouse.com

Published and distributed in Australia by:
Hay House Australia Ltd, 18/36 Ralph St, Alexandria NSW 2015. Tel.: (61) 2
9669 4299; Fax: (61) 2 9669 4144. www.hayhouse.com.au

Published and distributed in the Republic of South Africa by:
Hay House SA (Pty), Ltd, PO Box 990, Witkoppen 2068.
Tel./Fax: (27) 11 467 8904. www.hayhouse.co.za

Published and distributed in India by:
Hay House Publishers India, Muskaan Complex, Plot No.3, B-2, Vasant Kunj,
New Delhi – 110 070. Tel.: (91) 11 4176 1620; Fax: (91) 11 4176 1630.
www.hayhouse.co.in

Distributed in Canada by:
Raincoast, 9050 Shaughnessy St, Vancouver, BC V6P 6E5.
Tel.: (1) 604 323 7100; Fax: (1) 604 323 2600

A catalogue record for this book is available from the British Library.

ISBN 978-1-84850-155-3

Printed in the UK by CPI Bookmarque, Croydon CR0 4TD.

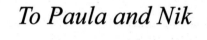

To Paula and Nik

Acknowledgements

An ancient African proverb says it takes a village to raise a child – but it also takes a village to write a book. I could not have written this book without my amazing band of mums in the village who have looked after me (brought me food/wine and love) and looked after my son Charlie and walked Oscar the dog while I was writing like a dervish. Massive thanks to Janine for leaving pies on my step and your loving support in the past year. Thanks to Siobhan, Viv, Nathalie, Karen, Laura, Cate, Seline, Emma, Alison, Sally for all your help, wise words, wine, inspiration and love.

To my Knights of the Round Table, I love you all: Nicky, Rachel, Nick M, Ros and Steve, Claire Power (and the lovely Barry), Louise, Lissen M and Michael B, Carolyn, Caroline and to the lovely Claire R for being a total star, and making me laugh when all I wanted to do was cry. You were round my table on my 40th and have been there for me in this mind-blowing year. I couldn't have leapt so far without you being by my side.

To the wonderful Georgia Foster and Viv Alves, my new business partners and fellow adventurers on the Big Peace journey. Thank you for your love and support.

Thank you to my amazing coaches Blaire Palmer, Rachel Pryor, Harriet Simon Salinger, Nick Williams, Arlene Mann, Gabriella Goddard – who have helped me leap at every step of the journey.

To Jacqueline Burns and Kirsty McLachlan, my publishing consultants and friends. Thank you for helping me shape my Big Peace idea and then sell it (www.publishabestseller.com).

Thank you to the lovely team at Hay House – Michelle Pilley, Jo Burgess, Meg Slyfield for believing in me and The Big Peace and my editors Barbara Vesey and Joanna Lincoln for helping me to make my manuscript sparkle.

Thanks to all my amazing Big Leaping clients who inspired me every day with their courage. Special thanks to all these Big Leapers who helped me compile all the inspirational quotes in this book: Marina Arnold, Alison Atwell, Dr. Magdalena Bak-Maier, Ken Barnes, Tracy Beattie, Tina Bernstein, Chris Booth, Paul Burbridge, Fariha Butt, Sharon Charlton-Thomson, Belinda Clarke, Ann Clifford, Nicky Coburn, Sharon Corbett, Liz Couch, Alison Cudmore, Victoria Cunningham, Siobhan Davies, Sophie Dixon, Donal Doherty, Michael Dooley, Deborah Downward, Brian Eccles, Kate England, Claire Findlater, Emma Freemantle, June Gatenby, Robert Grant, Victoria Green, Wendy Green, Frances Hall, Justina Hart, Nick Hatchard, Nicki Hill, Paula Hines, Gina Janssen, Carol Jerram, Sue Jobson, Diana Jordan, Angela Keogh, Lucinda Kidney, Emma King-Farlow, Alison Knapper, Sophie Komar, Tom Koukoulis, Wendy K Laidlaw Anderson, Gina Langton, Tracy Lepine, Lisa Letham, Sarah Little, Jan Louwris, Samantha Lowther, Liz MacNiven, Lyn Man, Alexia Marinides, Fleur Maule, Eilisha Mayhew, Judy Mihajlovic, Tessa Mills, Hayley Jayne Moore, Susan Moore, Nick Morgan, Sarah Navin, Kirsty Norton, Michele Nowell, Melanie O'Connor, Avril Oliver, Judy Oliver, Denise Parker, Jennie Peters, Kirstie Pursey, Suzanne Reynolds, Carole Ann Rice, Lindsey Riech, Marilyn Rieley, Tracey Rissik, Annie Ross Jones, Ian Savage, Tina Saxon, Ku Sharma, Cheryl Sharp, Jacqueline Skinner, Flora Skivington, Kristina Solem Wood, Kim Storks, Louise Sutherland, Zoë Street Howe, Nicola Summer, Anna Szelest, Carol Taylor, Karen Thipthorp, Anne Thorn, Michelle Venner, Sarah Wade, Marie Walsh, Tracey Weeks, Gary Young.

I could not do what I do without my Big Leap support team – a massive thank you to my Virtual Assistants Lesley Pringle and Emma Bibby (www.assistantguru.co.uk) for your unending support, your humour and love.

Thanks to Kate England for her beautiful cover design (www.marmalademoon.com)
And a huge thank you to all the experts and real 'gurus' out there who have inspired me and continue to inspire me on every step of my Big Peace journey.And finally, much love and thanks to my beautiful son Charlie and Oscar the dog. You light up my life and my left prefrontal lobe!

Contents

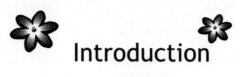

Introduction

'All I know is I'm losing my mind,' Franny said. 'I'm just sick of ego, ego, ego. My own and everyone else's. I'm sick of everybody that wants to get somewhere, do something distinguished and all, be someone interesting. It's disgusting – it is, it is. I don't care what anybody says ... I'm not afraid to compete. It's just the opposite. Don't you see that? I'm afraid I will compete – that's what scares me ... Just because I'm so horribly conditioned to accept everybody else's values, and just because I like applause and people to rave about me, doesn't make it right. I'm ashamed of it. I'm sick of it. I'm sick of not having the courage to be an absolute nobody. I'm sick of myself and everyone else that wants to make some kind of splash.' – **J D Salinger,** *Franny and Zooey*

The year 2007 started well for me – the *Daily Mail* named me as one of the top ten 'gurus' in the country – whatever that means – on New Year's Day. Just ten years earlier, on New Year's Day in 1997, I had woken up hungover and dribbling on a stranger's shoulder, as I had slept though my stop on the train. This catapulted me into making some big life changes: from being health editor of a glossy magazine to hiring a life coach – and then becoming one myself.

And here I was, a decade later, being hailed as a life-coaching 'guru'! Yes, my life was immeasurably better on every level – I had my lovely little four-year-old boy, a career I loved, money in the bank. So why, then, was I scanning the horizon for more? If I was supposed to be this clever-clogs 'guru', why did I feel so restless?

I started my Big Leap life-coaching business almost ten years ago. The focus had been on setting goals, achievement, creating 'the life you really want'. And it worked. My clients fronted prime-time TV shows, wrote best-selling books, created businesses and babies. And, as I supported my clients to make their leaps, I made my own. I established a successful life-coaching career, had a baby, built my business, moved to the country and wrote my book *Making the Big Leap*.

And that was wonderful. Goals were achieved, boxes were ticked, but what I noticed – in myself and in some of my clients – was that, once we'd achieved our goals, we were still itchy. We still wanted more. We were victims of what I call 'I'll be happy' thinking. ('I'll be happy when … I'm thinner/richer/more successful, achieved x, y, z,' etc.) And it was exhausting. So when I tried to set my goals for 2007, I completely stalled. What did I really, really want? I asked myself. I wanted to feel that inner peace, that sense of 'I'm there,' to be able to appreciate all that I had in my life without planning the next big thing.

So I set my 'goal' to 'find' my 'missing peace', and it's been – and still is – one of the most exciting journeys of my life.

The timing couldn't have been better. We are at a revolutionary point in history where we have an explosion of groundbreaking psychological research introducing the scientifically-based idea of 'positive psychology'.

The 'happiness scientists' are focusing for the first time on the question 'How can we be happy?' rather than the old model of 'How can we be less miserable?' and they are providing us with scientifically proven methods of cultivating contentment.

Science and spirituality have also begun to have an intelligent dialogue, as spiritual leaders such as the Dalai Lama meet some of the world's most distinguished scientists to discuss how humanity can become less destructive and more peaceful.

Combine this with the new pioneering science named 'neuroplasticity', which is revealing that the brain can change its wiring and its childhood emotional and genetic 'programming', and can alter its actual physical circuitry, if we think different thoughts and take different actions – and this was the perfect time to embark on my journey inward.

One of the most exciting discoveries I've made is that the decades of scientific research and dogma that said the brain was fixed in form and function have been overturned. It turns out that our brains are like gardens, and our neural pathways blossom the more time we spend tending them – be it practising a violin, which expands the part of the brain that controls the fingers, or restoring mental health by thinking thoughts in a different way.

Conversely, it's been found that if we *don't* take control of our thoughts and actions, weeds of negative and destructive thinking and behaviour can easily take over.

The good news is that the scientists say that, with consistent tending, we can vastly improve our 'set point' of happiness and peace of mind. It's what the self-development industry has been saying for years, but now we finally get a little scientific credibility – plus a host of new, proven, practical techniques. We do not have to be victims of our upbringing or even genetics – we can change our lives by thinking and doing differently. And that's without going anywhere. We can do it from the comfort of an armchair.

And that's where I've been for the last couple of years: On a journey without going away. Finding what I've come to call my 'big peace' from my armchair.

My background is in journalism, so I've had the privilege to interview some of the most influential self-development experts in the world and pick their brains – plus I have had access to the most cutting-edge scientific research on neuroplasticity and happiness.

With all this information I have developed a 90-day course that aims to bring together this research, new and ancient techniques, and ways to make your brain bloom with new, positive neural pathways.

What I've discovered is that you don't 'find' your Big Peace, you grow it. We are not stuck with the brain we were born or brought up with. We have the capacity to decide which functions will flower and which will wither – which emotions will blossom and which will die out.

So I'm going to throw all my (and others') best stuff at you – and hopefully you will exercise your brain a bit, which will actually change its structure, which in turn will make you feel calmer, lighter and generally more peaceful on the inside – no matter what drama is going on on the outside. So hopefully you will laugh more.

The Big Peace 90-day course is all about stopping all the effort, stress and jumping through hoops to be liked/successful/happy/thinner and living the 'I'll be happy when …' life, and starting instead to live in the creative present, where you can choose to be dynamic and fabulous right here, right now. All by changing your thinking.

I'm going to give you different techniques to try out day by day. Some of them are mine, some are adapted from people I consider to be the best self-development gurus in the world – everyone from Martha Beck (one of Oprah's favourite life coaches) to Dr David Hamilton (my favourite scientist).

It's quite a journey, and a process, to get focusing differently and ease yourself into a new way of being. And it's a journey with no destination. The Big Peace is not a place; it's a choice we make every second of every day. The Big Peace is a daily practice, so the good news is you're setting off on the journey but really you're already there. That's what I like – success before we've even set out!

My aim has been to create a practical guide to inner peace. I've read some very inspiring books and listened to some very inspiring people, but sometimes I've become frustrated because I couldn't figure out how to make what I was learning about part of my life in a practical way. The Big Peace is a very practical transformational course with daily tasks and practices to try. My hope is that you will find a handful of practices that you like and that can fit easily into your day, and so create a new positive practice for life.

This 90-day Big Peace course is not about self-improvement. We're not trying to make ourselves bigger, better, faster or richer. It's more about – dare I say it – loving ourselves and loving other people, too. With a great big dollop of self-acceptance.

And yes, that's accepting yourself right now, just as you are – with all your lumpy, bad, fabulous and brilliant bits – and all your nasty little habits, too.

We will be working from where you are right now – however awful you think you are. Sorry, there are no qualifications necessary to get on this programme. We're working with what we've got – with all our imperfections and ticks and tricks and bad childhoods, good childhoods ...

We all have histories – our personal tragedies, heartbreaks, rejections, our successes, love affairs, pain – that got us to wherever we are now. But that is the past. That is history.

The Big Peace is about living in the moment. Right here, right now. And working from that very second of Now – a very creative, dynamic moment in time. Because that moment is the moment of transformation, when you can choose to think or do things differently.

How to Read This Book: One Day at a Time

Over the next 90 days I'm going to be challenging you to think differently, asking you lots of questions and helping you to experiment with new theories and exercises to delve beneath your usual ways of thinking and allow you to try out different ways of being and doing.

This, in turn, will literally change the circuitry in your brain. My intention for the next 90 days is for us to have some fun, to experiment, to laugh at ourselves rather than judge ourselves and generally enjoy exploring a new world inside our heads.

I make the request that you don't read this book in one go. Instead, read and work through the exercises one day at a time. This book is a process, and nothing will change if you don't actually try out the exercises. I hope you will be able to do one task per day. If this is too much, then drop it down to one task per three days. I want you to be able to keep up the momentum but not be overwhelmed.

I've split the course into 12 weeks and have themed each week. Each week follows on from the next and, if you can, follow the course in sequence:

Week 1: Who do you think you are?
Week 2: Who do you want to be?
Week 3: Who's in charge?
Week 4: What's your story?
Week 5: What do you want?
Week 6: Are you happy now?
Week 7: How slow can you go?
Week 8: Are you willing to let it out?
Week 9: Are you willing to let go?
Week 10: Who loves ya, baby?
Week 11: What else?
Week 12: Who are you *not* to be?

There is one exercise to try per day. Try to stick to the programme if you can. But I'm going to make the assumption that you will read the days you need to read and find the right way for you. I want you to find a series of practices that you can make your own, that work for you. But obviously the more exercises you try, the better. Start from where you are and do the best with what you've got.

It may take only one of these exercises to change the way you think. So, if you're already thinking that this won't work for you, that you haven't got the stamina or patience to last 90 days, don't panic. The only rules in this book are:

The 5 Rules for Creating an Utterly Miserable Life or How NOT to Find Your Big Peace:

1. Strive to be perfect

Remind yourself at every occasion that you've got to get this perfectly right or you will never be approved of/loved/included or respected. That sounds like a fun way of going about things, doesn't it?

2. Compare yourself to others

By judging yourself and others, you'll get to feel either smug or crap (but how often will you really allow yourself to feel smug?).

3. Make happiness conditional

Constantly tell yourself, and others: 'I'll be happy when ... I'm thinner/richer/more successful', etc. You're putting your happiness on hold and living in fantasy land.

4. Try to prove that you're someone by pretending to be someone you're not.

A great strategy for constantly proving to yourself that you're not good enough as you are.

5. Spend all your time and energy trying to make someone else happy.

Some of the time, perhaps? But notice how much energy you spend focusing on other people's lives – mind your own business!

Week 1

Who Do You Think You Are?

'This is your last chance. After this, there is no turning back. You take the blue pill – the story ends, you wake up in your bed and believe whatever you want to believe. You take the red pill – you stay in Wonderland and I show you how deep the rabbit-hole goes.' **– Morpheus talking to Neo in the film *The Matrix***

In Week 1 we're going to explore what we think about ourselves and life. When I first started on my coaching journey and hired my very first life coach, I didn't realize I had an opinion – and then discovered the profound effect that my hidden opinion was having on my life. At the time, I had no clue.

I was a journalist, working 16 hours a day, using coffee to get me up, cigarettes to keep me going and alcohol to make me stop (and I was a health editor for a national magazine!). I turned up to my coaching session moaning about life, about how tired I was.

My coach asked me to focus on what I *did* want versus what I did not.

'What would a life you adored really look like?', my coach asked. A life I adored? At first I sneered, but I decided to humour my coach and mentioned lots of time off, a loving relationship, a baby, a job that I loved.

Then came a question that changed my life: 'What would you have to believe about yourself for this dream to come true?' I blustered, I sneered a bit more, but in the end I wept. I realized that, for me to get a life I adored, the thing that was going to have to change was me. I didn't believe I was good enough to manifest even a tiny piece of a dream life.

Through my own journey, and now from coaching hundreds of my own clients, I have discovered that our beliefs and the stories we tell ourselves drive our lives. If you don't believe you're good enough, you can't say no, you put up with stuff you don't want to put up with, and you work all day and night to prove that you are worthy of a place in the world.

Over and over again I see my clients people-pleasing, spending time with people they don't even like, working like dogs just to buy clothes, cars and houses to prove to themselves and to others that they're somebody. Twelve years ago, that was me. It's not surprising I was tired – I spent my whole life in an exhausting pantomime that actually had nothing to do with what I wanted and everything to do with my fears of who I thought I wasn't.

Of course, there's a pay-off for living that kind of life: It keeps you safe. You don't have to go after your dreams. You can blame everyone else – your husband, your stressful job, your fascist boss – for your crap life. You can moan and grumble about your life and *you don't have to do anything about it*. You can keep your macho pride about how 'stressed' you are, and remain a martyr to the cause.

I didn't know any other way to live. Up until that point, life had happened to me. I had muddled through and I didn't realize I had a choice. And there I was in my first session being asked to take responsibility, to be the creator of my life rather than the victim of it.

And as scary as that was, it was also incredibly empowering.

Over the next couple of weeks I'm going to ask you become the creator of your thoughts instead of their victim. This week, we're going to be doing lots of exercises so you can simply become aware of your thoughts and beliefs and how they drive your life. I will be encouraging you to step back one inch so you can observe your thoughts rather than be in them.

Big Peace Day 1: Do 15 Minutes of Nothing

'I am so busy doing nothing ... that the idea of doing anything – which as you know, always leads to something – cuts into the nothing and then forces me to have to drop everything.' – Jerry Seinfeld

Your 'task' today is simple: I want you to do 15 minutes of nothing.

You can lie down, sit, but all I need you to do is – nothing. Find somewhere where you won't be disturbed and where you can be alone.

As you sit there/fall asleep/dribble, notice the conversation you are having with yourself. You don't literally have to be talking out loud to yourself, because some people think this makes you nuts, but I do need you to observe the thoughts you have about this 'task' – and write them down.

Be it 'I do nothing all the time, this programme is obviously not for me but for stressed-out executives who are burnt out, not for layabout nobodies like me' or 'Fifteen minutes of doing nothing? Are you insane? I'm far too busy to take 15 minutes out of my diary – I've got to have a conference call with Hong Kong/cook the kids' dinner/go to the gym/do the online supermarket shop/learn how to wrestle with crocodiles.'

Notice your thoughts, that's all.

Big Peace Day 2: Observing Thought Bubbles

'Begin by taming your own mind.' – **Buddha**

How did you get on with your 15 minutes of nothing? If you found this 'task' very difficult (or perhaps you haven't done it yet?), that's OK. I simply need you to start observing your thoughts.

Today, I want you to ask yourself: What is a thought? Where does it come from? Is it real? Ponder these questions for a moment.

I want you to get used to the idea of observing what you think about yourself, of noticing your inner experience. I must admit the first time I did this I was fairly alarmed and immediately started judging myself: 'I am nuts. I am so negative. If people knew what I was thinking, they'd lock me up.'

So don't be worried at first if you find yourself having a dialogue about your inner dialogue. Just go back to observing your thoughts – as if you were merely describing a scene inside a character's head in a novel.

With a pen and paper, start observing your thoughts – totally non-judgementally, as if they were in a thought bubble. Write down what you see or hear in that bubble and then let it float away. You can draw bubbles on your page and write your thoughts within them, if that helps.

Let me share with you my thought bubbles from this morning:

'I'm hungry.' 'My leg hurts.' 'I've got to get some more dog food.' 'I haven't made the bed yet.' 'I need some more support.' 'I'm tired.' 'If only x would help me more.' 'Maybe I just need to ask.' 'I need the loo.' 'I need to clean the bathroom.' 'Ah, Oscar looks so sweet sleeping there.' 'Look how muddy he is.' 'He really smells.' 'I should bath him.' 'I wonder if I can sort out a dog bath for the summer outside?' 'What do other people do who have dogs?' 'Do their dogs smell?' 'What if my house smells?' 'I must remember to ask someone if my house smells.' 'I should be more house-proud.' 'Oh, I'm doing OK.' 'I'm not.' 'I'm tired.' 'I can smell something.' 'What is that smell?' 'Urgh!' 'That bloody dog.' 'I should get up and clean up.' 'Why am I just sitting here?' 'This isn't working.' 'A bubble.' 'A thought bubble.' 'Watch it.' 'I love bubbles.' 'I need to buy some of that fantastic bubble bath.' 'I need to have a bath every night with bubbles.' 'I need to clean the bath.' 'It would be great to get a cleaner.' 'Can I afford it?' 'I need to do my budgeting.' 'I should do it.' 'I'm supposed to be a grown-up.' 'I'm so crap.' 'I'm not.' 'I'm doing OK.' 'I'm cold.' 'I love my new quilt.' 'I want to buy another one for the other bed.' 'I'll have to stop the dog going upstairs.' 'There are definitely paw prints on this quilt.' 'Oscar, he's so sweet.' 'Oscar.' 'I love Oscar.' 'Urgh! You smell, Oscar.' 'I'm sick of this.' 'Is it 15 minutes yet?' 'What am I doing again?' 'A thought bubble.'

And that, dear friends, was only five minutes of thoughts. You see? And you thought *you* were insane. I'm joking, because this is not about judging yourself. It is simply allowing yourself to step back and observe what is going on.

Next question – If you are not your thoughts, who are you? Who is the person doing the observing?

Perhaps you don't care. But being able to observe your thoughts instead of being *in* them is a pretty powerful skill to tuck into your backpack on your journey to 'find' the Big Peace. Because this kind of exercise – where one observes one's thoughts versus reacting to them – has been shown not only to help change old, peace-robbing behaviours but actually to change the structure of the brain.

Neuro-psychiatrist Jeffrey Schwartz of the University of California, Los Angeles launched a behaviour-therapy group to study and treat Obsessive Compulsive Disorder (OCD). Patients with OCD show an unusually high activity in the part of the brain that triggers fear reactions.

Schwartz, a practising Buddhist, became intrigued with the therapeutic practice of *mindfulness* – where you stand outside your own mind, observing the spontaneous thoughts and feelings the brain spews out, observing this as if it were happening to someone else.

Working with 18 OCD patients, who had moderate to severe symptoms, Schwartz would show them scans of their brains overreacting fearfully on an MRI scan. Over ten weeks of therapy, Schwartz taught his patients to use mindfulness to focus on the new thought that their compulsions were not actually 'them', but misfiring brain circuitry.

The patients came to understand that they didn't need to wash their hands obsessively but were instead just witnessing the arrival of an obsessive thought. Out of 18 patients, 12 improved significantly and stopped their old behaviours. Using a brain-imaging technique, the scientists found that their brains had become structurally normal.

The brain that observes itself changes itself. Try it today.

Big Peace 3: Don't Get Eaten by a Lion

'Sometimes, if you stand on the bottom rail of a bridge and lean over to watch the river slipping slowly away beneath you, you will suddenly know everything there is to know.' – **Winnie the Pooh**

More variation on the same theme today. Try out this wonderful exercise from the renowned meditation teacher and writer, Stephen Levine, who talks about seeing our thoughts as boxcars on a freight train.

Levine asks us to imagine standing at a railway crossing, watching a freight train passing by. He challenges us to try to keep looking ahead into the present, rather than being pulled towards looking into each of the carriages:

'As we attend to the train, we notice there's supper in one boxcar, but we just ate, so we're not pulled by that one.

'The laundry list is the next one, so we reflect for a moment on the blue towel hanging on the line to dry, but we wake up quite quickly to the present once again, as the next boxcar has someone in it meditating and we recall what we're doing.

'A few more boxcars go by with thoughts clearly recognized as thoughts. But, in the next one is a snarling lion chasing someone who looks like us. We stay with that one until it's way down the line to see if it gets us. We identify with that one because it "means" something to us. We have an attachment to it.

'Then we notice we've missed all the other boxcars streaming by in the meantime and we let go of our fascination for the lion and bring our attention straight ahead into the present once again.'

I loved this description of the way our thoughts work. Without the instruction or intention to keep our eyes straight ahead on the present, how many of us realize that we have a choice?

How many of us remember that we can simply focus on another carriage – the one with the supper or the laundry list in it? Or simply focus on looking straight ahead into the present?

How many of us realize that whatever we put our attention on can eat us up, be it a lion or a thought?

Negative thoughts are like snarling lions – they have us hooked when we focus on them. So we end up wrestling the lion because, if we don't, we think he'll eat us.

The irony is that the more we wrestle and fight the thoughts about the lion, the more power we give them. However, to step outside and be able to observe our thoughts dissolves their power. 'That isn't really a lion, that's just a thought about a lion.' Ping, the lion disappears.

Today, try this exercise for another 15 minutes. See if you can observe your thoughts as train carriages.

Big Peace Day 4: What Do You Think about Yourself?

'The real voyage of discovery consists not in seeking new landscapes but in having new eyes.' – **Marcel Proust**

Yesterday we were observing our thoughts, which might make it easier to answer the question today: What do you believe about yourself?

When observing your thoughts, is there a theme that shines through? From my 'bubble notes' on Day 2, you can probably see that I have a very smelly dog. But I noticed, too, that there was a theme about lack of support. Do I believe I deserve or can ask for help? There's something there about money, too.

Today we're going to tackle the first step in changing our beliefs: Identifying the beliefs that are driving our life.

What do your thought bubbles tell you? Do you believe that life is wonderful, that you will always be OK, that you are priceless, that you deserve only the best and that life is easy? Do you believe you will always be supported and you always land on your feet, that life is fun, that you always attract the best in life and life is one big party?

Or do you believe that life is hard, money is the root of all evil, all men are bastards, all women are mad, life is a struggle, men don't commit, life is a rollercoaster, all men leave, all women cheat, and that you have to be bad to be rich? Do you believe you'll never make it because you're not good enough, in fact you're actually pretty worthless – oh, and you're stupid, too?

What is your reality? What do you believe to be true about yourself and your life? The good and bad news (depending on what you believe) is that you're right. Because whatever you believe, you're right. The woman who believes that all men cheat and life's a bitch and then you die is right. The man who believes all women are angels and life is a lifelong party is right, too. What you focus on expands.

So it makes sense to create a belief structure and thinking pattern that help you rather than hinder you. And the good news is that it's just a matter of some mental training.

Even better news – it's been proven to work. Scientists have found that cognitive behavioural therapy (CBT) – a form of mental training therapy developed in the 1960s to help patients struggling with depression – works just as well as anti-depressants.

With CBT, patients are taught to think differently and change negative beliefs to more positive, life-affirming thoughts – for example, 'A lousy date means I'm a failure as a human being' would be changed to 'My lousy date was just one of those things that didn't work out.'

Training a patient to replace negative thoughts and 'catastrophic' thinking to more helpful, positive thinking resulted in patients not spiralling into negative thoughts and depression.

Other research shows that this approach works because you are literally training the brain to adopt different thinking circuits, reshaping how you process information in the cortex, the thinking part of the brain. So not only will thinking differently make you feel better, it literally changes the physical make-up of your brain.

But we're getting ahead of ourselves. First things first. Let's discover what you believe.

Do your fundamental beliefs about yourself and your life help or hinder you?

Answer these questions and let's see if we can winkle out an idea of what you really believe about

yourself and life. Just quickly put pen to paper –
don't think too hard, and speed-write your answers.

- ❀ What decision did you have to make to survive
  and thrive in your family?
- ❀ What happens to people like you?
- ❀ What will people say about you when you are
  dead?
- ❀ What negative feeling do you feel most often?
- ❀ When you get this feeling, what do you believe
  about yourself?
- ❀ When you get this feeling, what do you believe
  about life?
- ❀ What do you believe about yourself to have a
  career like yours?
- ❀ What would you have to believe about yourself
  to have a relationship history like yours?
- ❀ What would you have to believe about yourself
  to have a circle of friends like yours?
- ❀ What would you have to believe about yourself,
  or life, for things to be exactly as they are right
  now?

Put these questions and answers away for now; we'll
come back to them a little later on. For now, ask
yourself this: What effect do your current beliefs
have on your life?

Big Peace Day 5: What Do You Need?

'We should not be embarrassed by our difficulties, only our failure to grow anything beautiful from them.' – Alain de Botton

Yesterday we looked at the *beliefs* from your past that may be driving you in your present. Today we're going to be travelling back in time and identifying any *emotional needs* that might be driving you as well.

Emotional needs are a very strong driving force in our lives. Most of my clients first turn up to coaching because one of their emotional needs is not getting met. And unmet needs are the greatest peace-robbers around, so it's important we know how to get them met.

Emotional needs are usually formed in childhood, where we made decisions and created behaviour patterns in order to get what we needed at the time and keep us safe – which then spill over into our adult lives.

For example, as a grown-up you may have an emotional need to 'fit in' because as a five-year-old you were bullied by Johnny Bailey because you were 'trying to be different' when you turned up in the playground wearing your new day-glo socks. When our emotional needs are met, we feel at peace, at one with the world, generous, expanded. If you have a need to fit in and are fitting in beautifully, then you feel king of the hill. But woe betide if you don't.

Unmet needs feel like being permanently hungry – they make you feel irritable and snappy, and if your needs go unmet for long enough, it can make you feel as if you are emotionally starving.

It's much easier to live a peaceful life with a metaphorical full stomach, otherwise you waste a lot of energy scouring the world for leftovers. And sometimes if you're so starving for your needs to be met, you end up down blind alleys, rifling through bins for scraps.

You may not like the word 'needy'. It's usually spat out as an insult – the more 'needless' you appear, the more emotionally healthy you are perceived to be. But that's a dangerous concept to buy, because unless you're some kind of enlightened being, you will have emotional needs. Deny your emotional needs and they become like hidden addictions. You will do anything to get your fix.

Whether you work 16 hours a day to meet your need to be accepted by your boss or eat maggots on a trash TV show to meet your need for acclaim, you should never underestimate the heights of miserable or bizarre behaviour that you can and will sink to when trying to get your emotional needs met.

Many an addiction is propping up an unmet emotional need. If you find yourself overeating, smoking or drinking, you are most likely trying to anaesthetize the pain of your unmet needs.

One of the reasons why many of us find it difficult to stop our bad habits has nothing to do with the addictive quality of the substance itself, but everything to do with trying to avoid feeling the pain of an unmet need. It is kinder to yourself to stop trying to give up your habits until you finish the process of getting your needs met, as it will feel much easier then.

So, today, we are going to work on identifying what your possible unmet needs might be.

Let's travel back in time for a moment, and consider these questions:

❀ As a child, what behaviour earned you 'brownie points'?

❀ As a child, what behaviour earned you disapproval?

❀ What decisions did you make as a child to survive and thrive in your family?

Now, back in the present, think about:

❀ How are those decisions showing up in your life now as an adult?

❀ What effect are those decisions having on your life now?

17

❧ What decisions could you now make differently so you will be able to survive and thrive as an adult?

Most of the time, we're not even aware that our emotional needs are driving our behaviour. We will, however, recognize when we're unhappy, depressed, irritable, sad, jealous, angry or feeling unloved or unappreciated.

Today, whenever you are feeling down, ask yourself:

❧ At this moment in time, what is it that I'm not getting that I need?

Is it a hug, praise, respect, control of a situation, acknowledgement, approval, to be heard, security, inspiration, success, to be loved? You fill in the blanks.

Tomorrow we'll go into more detail about this. For now, just keep asking that question.

Big Peace Day 6: What's Your Need?

'To live is the rarest thing, most just survive.'
– Oscar Wilde

Today I want you to read the following statements and see if you can identify your unmet needs. There are hundreds of different needs, but there are some common 'groups' of needs and yours might be a version of one of these.

Is your answer 'Yes' to three or more of these statements?
✿ I become tense when someone is late.
✿ I become annoyed by others' sloppy standards
✿ I am a tidy and methodical person.
✿ I can get snappy with disorganized people.
✿ I like to have possession of the remote control.
Possible unmet need: to be right, to be perfect, to be in control.

Is your answer 'Yes' to three or more of these statements?
✿ I'm always exhausted because I tend to be rushing around helping my friends out.
✿ I know instinctively how to make people feel good.
✿ I make lots of effort to find out what is going on in the lives of friends and family so I can be there for them.
✿ I feel outraged and resentful if people don't appreciate me.
✿ I send thoughtful presents and cards to friends and colleagues just to let them know I'm thinking of them.

Possible unmet need: to be approved of, to be needed, to be loved, to be cherished, to be liked.

Is your answer 'Yes' to three or more of these statements?

❀ When things are going well for me, I literally light up inside.

❀ I will work very long hours to ensure something is a success.

❀ I'd rather die than be a failure.

❀ I'm really aware how friends and colleagues are doing and can be quite competitive.

❀ I am great at achieving goals.

❀ I have workaholic tendencies – I feel tense inside if I'm not accomplishing what I set out to do.

Possible unmet need: to achieve, to be successful, to feel worthwhile, to be accepted.

Is your answer 'Yes' to three or more of these statements?

❀ If I'm criticized or misunderstood, I sulk.

❀ People say I can be difficult and too emotional, but what's wrong with that?

❀ I know how to make a really big scene if I don't get what I want.

❀ Rules are meant to be broken.

❀ I tend to brood a lot about my negative feelings.

Possible unmet need: for acclaim, to be special, to be different, to be heard, to be understood.

Is your answer 'Yes' to three or more of these statements?
- ❄ I'm an expert in my area.
- ❄ I love to study something in depth and really get my teeth stuck into it.
- ❄ I am the eternal student.
- ❄ I often lose track of time because I get carried away with what I'm doing.
- ❄ I won't try something new until I'm confident that I know everything I need to know.

Possible unmet need: to be competent, to be the expert, to be capable.

Is your answer 'Yes' to three or more of these statements?
- ❄ Anxiety is my middle name.
- ❄ I worry about everything, everybody and his dog.
- ❄ I like having a boss I can respect.
- ❄ I find it difficult to make a decision without asking all my friends, my parents and my colleagues first.
- ❄ It takes me ages to make a change to another job.

Possible unmet need: for security, for safety, for support, for certainty.

Is your answer 'Yes' to three or more of these statements?

❀ I get bored easily.

❀ I'm curious about stuff.

❀ I love travelling and having fabulous holidays.

❀ I am all over the place most of the time – people think I'm a bit dizzy.

❀ I always feel like I'm missing out on things – the grass is always greener on the other side for me.

Possible unmet need: to be stimulated, to be free, to be satisfied, to have adventures, to be excited.

Is your answer 'Yes' to three or more of these statements?

❀ I like to challenge people. No one could call me a shrinking violet.

❀ I tend to have huge temper tantrums.

❀ I am independent and don't like people trying to tie me down.

❀ I don't rely on anyone.

❀ I love trying to achieve the impossible.

Possible unmet need: to protect yourself, to determine your own course in life.

Is your answer 'Yes' to three or more of these statements?

❧ I'm one of life's peacemakers – I can't bear a scene.

❧ There's no point dwelling on the negative – is there?

❧ I like my home comforts.

❧ Most people tend to get too worked up about the little things – what's the point?

❧ I go with the flow.

Possible unmet need: for calm, for agreement, for steadiness, for peace.

What unmet needs did you identify with? You may have two or three, maybe more. For now, write them down. We'll work out how to fulfil these needs in the next couple of days.

Big Peace Day 7: Fulfilling Your Unmet Emotional Needs

'Peace of mind is attained not by ignoring problems, but by solving them.' – **Raymond Hull**

Once you've identified your emotional needs, it's now time to work out a strategy to get them fulfilled in a healthier way – rather than sulking to get your need for attention met, or eating kangaroo genitalia on national TV because you have a need for acclaim!

You will need help from others to do this, although, ironically, we often unconsciously surround ourselves with the very people who *cannot* meet our emotional needs. You will need to choose people who care and love you enough to help you do this, so create your need-meeting team carefully. If you're struggling to think of a team, then just choose one person.

Try this exercise today:

❀ Choose a team of friends and family who would be willing to help you meet your needs.
❀ Explain to them about the concept of unmet needs.
❀ Choose the unmet need with the most 'symptoms', so you can recognize it most easily.
❀ Create a Needs-fulfilment Project and give your team specific and measurable things to do or say to get your need met.

For example, if you have a need for approval, get them to email you every day with another reason why they like or love you so much, or arrange an appointment with your boss and explain that the best way to get optimum results with you is to praise you rather than criticize you.

This exercise is very challenging. The problem with our unmet needs is that we assume people know what we need and are in some way choosing to withhold their love, support or praise. That's not the case – they simply don't know what our needs are. (If they do know, you need to ask yourself why you are spending time with these people in the first place.)

This exercise will help you discover how great it feels to get your needs met. I remember feeling like I was king of the hill as friends would leave a message or send an email telling me how much they loved me. I know it sounds sappy, but try it. It is an incredibly transformational exercise.

The downside with this exercise is that we're looking outside ourselves to feel better on the inside. But this is Week 1, and it's our starting point. This exercise will help you experience how getting your needs met makes you feel more peaceful. We will do more inner work in Weeks 3 and 4 on how you can do this all by yourself. For now, ask for help. And experience what it feels like to get your needs met.

Week 2

Who Do You Want to Be?

'You are today where your thoughts have brought you; you will be tomorrow where your thoughts take you.' – James Allen

So in your first week of the programme you began to discover (or perhaps confirm what you already knew about) the beliefs, recurring thoughts and unmet needs that are driving your life.

Over the next week I want to introduce several techniques that will help you to retrain your brain to make the leap from old ways of thinking to a new way of thinking.

This, in turn, will start building new neural pathways in your brain.

Norman Doidge, psychiatrist and psychoanalyst, compares the brain to a muscle in his groundbreaking book *The Brain That Changes Itself*. The more you exercise the muscle, the bigger it gets. It's like the old adage: If you don't use it, you lose it. Studies have shown that when we change our thought processes, we literally grow a blossoming new network of neurons and connections in our brains – and the old networks wither and die.

Another old adage springs to mind: What we focus on expands. And exercising my brain in this way certainly changed my life.

I was working very long hours, saying 'Yes' to every task and assignment in my job as a journalist. My coach asked me, 'What's beneath that?' 'Well, I'm not a very good writer,' I said. 'I'm not good enough, I've got to work very hard and over-deliver or they'll find out I'm no good.'

'Is that really true?' asked my coach. 'Where's the evidence?' 'Er …' I couldn't think of any evidence, but I just *knew* it to be true. She asked me to create a physical 'wall of evidence' that I was a good writer – to find a wall in my house and stick up the articles that I had written – all of them.

So I did – one by one. There were four-page spreads in the *Daily Mail*, lead features in *Marie Claire*, the *Sunday Times*, the *Express*, the *Mirror*, *Zest* magazine, *Cosmopolitan* magazine and many more. When I was finished, practically the whole wall was full of magazine and newspaper articles. 'If you weren't good at writing, why would these national newspapers and magazines be hiring you – not just once but over and over again?' asked my coach.

Good question. I literally felt something shift. 'Maybe I am quite good,' I thought. Over a few weeks, I felt my confidence shift and I started to be able to say 'No' to the jobs I didn't want to do, to ask for more money and eventually to apply for the job of health editor of *New Woman*, which was 'magazine of the year' that year. And they accepted me. I then went on to be health editor of *OK!* magazine. That small shift – created by questioning my old thoughts with a new body of evidence – created more peace and self-confidence in my life – and more success.

> When you face yourself with concrete evidence and focus differently, a negative belief can disintegrate in seconds.

This week you will be creating your own 'wall of evidence' to back up the new beliefs that you wish to adopt.

You're going to be deciding which new positive thought you'd like to plant and grow in the 'gardens' of your mind, and which thoughts you'd like to weed out. But, as with a blossoming garden, this does take work and constant tending.

Right, get your wellies on and let's get started.

Big Peace Day 8: What Would You Like to Think about Yourself?

'I am the greatest. I said that even before I knew I was. Don't tell me I can't do something. Don't tell me it's impossible. Don't tell me I'm not the greatest. I'm the double greatest.' – Muhammad Ali

We've started to explore what you already do think about yourself. This week we're going to look at what you'd *like* to think about yourself.

You may have a few ideas, but today I'm giving you a few new belief systems to play with – and let's see what happens.

Sometimes I think it's easier to act our way into a new way of thinking, so let's choose one of the following beliefs/thoughts, try it on for size, and act as if it were already true for the next 24 hours.

Make it your minute-by-minute mantra. Remember that you've been thinking one way all your life, so at first this might feel like trying to rub your stomach and pat your head at the same time – but today we're just experimenting with how it feels to live by a different belief structure. And it can be really good fun.

OK ... choose one of these beliefs and play with a new reality for 24 hours:

1   I'm great.
2   I'm a very attractive human being.
3   I'm not perfect but I'm lovely.
4   This too shall pass.
5   This present is exactly as it's supposed to be.
6   I'm OK just the way I am.
7   I'm sexy.
8   I'm a creative genius.
9   I embrace change.
10 My potential is limitless.

Today, ask yourself: If you could really believe this statement, how would you act differently, talk differently, walk differently, think differently? Try it out today.

Big Peace Day 9: Create an Evidence Wall

'The outer conditions of a person's life will always be found to reflect their inner beliefs.' – James Allen

I hope you had fun yesterday. Did that technique work for you? Do you think that it's something you can adopt as your Big Peace practice? What changes did you find yourself making? What did you do differently? How did adopting a new belief system manifest physically in your life? Were you calmer?

Were you braver? Did you start writing a novel? Ask a stranger on a date? Notice what worked for you.

Today we're going to do more of the same, but in a different way. You're going to create a new belief of your own and start to create your own 'wall of evidence'.

First, I want you to identify the belief you would like to adopt to create a more peaceful life – for example, 'I am good enough,' 'Everything always works out in the end,' 'I am loved.'

What do you need to believe to live a peaceful life?

Don't worry if your brain grinds to a halt and you go blank. You are going to be literally creating a new 'thought pathway' in your brain, and usually the old belief has a neural groove that is well worn, so this is not easy at first.

Ask yourself: What ten pieces of evidence can you find that prove that this new belief is true?

For example, if the belief you want to implant is 'I can handle everything that life throws at me,' your evidence might include: 'I'm not dead yet! I haven't collapsed in a heap yet; I'm actually quite good in a crisis (state example); when Monty hurt his paw I knew what to do and stayed very calm. When Mum died, I sorted everything out,' etc., etc.

You can either create a physical 'evidence wall' like I did – stick up pictures, statements, photographs on a wall which prove that your new belief is true. Or just start creating a list in a notepad. If after ten pieces of evidence your list looks skimpy or the wall looks a bit bare, start looking for five ways every day to prove that this new belief is true. What you focus on expands. The more you look for something, the more you will find it, the more your wall of evidence will grow.

From working with clients I've discovered that, at around the 50-pieces-of-evidence mark, an old belief starts to crumble round the edges (you may feel resistance at this point). Keep going until you reach the magic 100 and the old belief will disintegrate altogether. It's more challenging at the beginning, but once you start the new belief builds momentum and you start to notice all sorts of additional evidence that your new belief is true.

This is usually because your external circumstances begin to change as you make different decisions – and you may find yourself working less, earning more, surrounding yourself with loving, supportive people, taking risks and doing something you love versus what you ought. This in turn builds more evidence for your wall that what you believe is true. It's a very powerful process.

Big Peace Day 10: What Will You Say No To?

'Emancipate yourself from mental slavery; none but ourselves can free our mind.' – Bob Marley

When you start building a new belief system, you may find that you want to change some of the systems (or even the people) that you have around you.

So today, a short coaching question: **What would you have to give up or change if you were to fully embody your new belief system?**

For example, if you truly believed you were good enough, what would you say 'No' to? If you believed that everything was going to work out, what would you do with the energy that you used to worry with? If you believed it was possible to change your life versus be the victim of it, what would you simply not tolerate in your life? If you believed you were loved, what habits could you give up? Who would you stop spending time with? What would you stop doing? Spend 15 minutes today with a paper and pad and answer those questions.

Big Peace Day 11: New Rules for Living

'One of the very first things I figured out about life ... is that it's better to be a hopeful person than a cynical, grumpy one, because you have to live in the same world either way, and if you're hopeful, you have more fun.' – **Barbara Kingsolver**

Another short coaching question today: As you start to build your evidence wall, ask yourself: **If you were to live and embody your new belief system, what five new standards would you want to live your life by?**

For example, 'I only hang around with people who are supportive and kind,' 'I'm going to stop focusing on the future and always ask myself what I can do right now, right here,' 'I'm going to give up complaining and focus on what I'm grateful for.'

I loved Will Bowen's book *How to Stop Complaining and Start Enjoying the Life You Always Wanted* – and his 21-day challenge. A pastor in America, he got fed up with people moaning about their lives, so issued a challenge to swear off complaining, criticizing, gossiping or using sarcasm for 21 days.

People who joined in got a purple bracelet as a reminder of their pledge to stop complaining. If they caught themselves complaining, they were supposed to take off the bracelet, switch it to the opposite wrist and start counting the days from scratch.

I'm not suggesting you stop complaining today, simply that you create a new standard to live your life by that feels life-affirming and gets you focusing on what you want rather than what you don't want. You don't have to wear a purple bracelet if you don't want to!

Big Peace Day 12: Is It True?

'The primary cause of unhappiness is never the situation but your thoughts about it. Separate thoughts from the situation, which is always as it is.'
– Eckhart Tolle

Over the next few days I want to introduce you to another change to your thinking process. It is a brilliant, portable tool that you can use to challenge old beliefs in the moment, with the simple question – *is it true?*

This question is from 'The Work', a simple but effective process created by Byron Katie, author of *Loving What Is* and lauded as 'a visionary for the New Millennium' by *Time* magazine.

Katie has created a simple four-question process which allows you to question your beliefs (or what

I call the peace-robbing thoughts) which steal our peace of mind.

First, identify a belief or thought that is making you feel miserable. For example, my thought might be: 'Paul is unsupportive.'

Now work through this process with me, step by step.

'Paul is unsupportive to me.'

❋ *1. Is it true?*
What's the reality of the situation? When I first started working with this process, I would always scream at this point, 'Yes, yes, of course, it's true. Paul is incredibly unsupportive,' and I would ring all my girlfriends to force them to agree with me so I could tell them another reason why Paul was so unsupportive. We would tut and suck our teeth. 'Mmmm. So unsupportive,' we'd say.
So I always hated the second question of Katie's process.

❋ *2. Can you know absolutely that it's true?*
'Can you absolutely know the truth about another person?' asks Katie.
This part of the questioning process just gets you to stop and reflect for a moment, which unfortunately will mean leaving my aggrieved 'I'm right' teeth-sucking opinions aside for a moment.

Can I really know that Paul is being unsupportive to me? Well, I can't really know. I'm not Paul. I can't see into his mind or heart. Was he just being a bit vague? Maybe he had his own problems that day and wasn't really listening.

❊ *3. How do you react when you think that thought? (… that Paul is unsupportive)*
I feel unloved, enraged, angry, sad, resentful (I support him all the time …!), bitter, twisted, I suck my teeth, I'm aggrieved, p**sed off. Shall I go on? Usually I'm snarling at this point.
'Mmm,' says Katie. 'Can you find one stress-free reason to keep the thought that Paul is unsupportive to you?'
Stress-free reason to keep thinking the thought that Paul is unsupportive? Looking at the stressed-out list above, none whatsoever.
(Can you see what is happening here? Can you see why this process is so brilliant? It questions your thoughts, challenges the way YOU think versus having a conversation about the unsupportive Paul.)

❊ *4. Who would you be without that thought?*
This question always makes my brain take a deep breath. 'How would your life be different in the same situation without this thought?' asks Katie.

Well, I would see Paul just being Paul getting on
with his life, and I wouldn't be jumping up and
down on my hat having a tantrum. On the contrary,
without the thought that he is unsupportive, I
wouldn't be angry or resentful towards him. I would
appreciate him a lot more.

Today, I want you to use the above process. Identify
a peace-robbing thought and then use the process
above to question it.

Tomorrow we'll do a bit more on this.

Big Peace Day 13: Think a Peaceful Thought

*'When I let go of what I am, I become what I might
be.'* – Laozi

Today we're going to try what Byron Katie calls 'the
turnaround'. This where we take that peace-robbing
thought and experience its opposite.

'Find an opposite to your original statement,' says
Katie.

Sometimes it's the direct opposite, i.e. 'Paul is
unsupportive' turns into 'Paul is supportive to me.'
Then you're asked to find at least three specific,
genuine examples of how that turnaround is true
in your life. How might it be true that Paul is
supportive?

At first you might be too angry or upset to open your mind to examples. But if you take a good look, you can find them, even if they're small examples. For example, 'He hasn't left me. He says "Good morning" to me. He takes out the garbage.'

Actually, what works better for me on this turnaround is: '*I* am unsupportive to me.'

How am I unsupportive to myself? Oh, let me count the ways. I can find three in a flash.

Another turnaround: 'I am unsupportive to Paul.'

Yes, that is true as well. Finding examples might be hard when I am feeling resentful, but I can certainly find them.

So find a statement that you can turn around which hits you between the eyes and feels very true.

I love this process because it gives me a very quick way to question my thoughts when I find myself sucking my teeth and complaining. And within minutes I can be in a calmer, more resourceful state.

I think Byron Katie's 'The Work' is one of the most powerful and liberating exercises you can do. Check out her website www.thework.com and download her free worksheets. Or sign up to her buddy system, where you can work with a buddy for a whole month dismantling your aggro belief systems one by one.

Big Peace Day 14: Affirm!

'It takes but one positive thought when given a chance to survive and thrive to overpower an entire army of negative thoughts.' – **Robert Schuller**

Today, let's finish Week 2 with some affirmations – positive statements we say out loud.

We have been focusing on what we want to believe, but unless we tend our new shoots with the right kind of fertilizer, water them and protect them from early frosts, they may die off before they take hold. Think of affirmations as like manure for those new thinking-shoots.

Why do affirmations work? 'Our thoughts have an astonishing effect on our bodies,' says Dr David Hamilton, author of *How Your Mind Can Heal Your Body*.

Hamilton is my favourite scientist – inspired by field research tests he conducted for drug companies, he realized that placebo tests produce comparable results to those achieved by actual medications, and he set about trying to understand why. 'The more research I did, the more studies I found that showed irrefutable evidence that the thoughts we think have a massive impact on our healing capacity.'

Affirmations work, Hamilton says, because when

we say something over and over again, we create neural connections in the brain. The more we say it, the more connections we create and the stronger they become.

Dr Hamilton says: 'Talking about your hand activates the hand area of the brain. Therefore repeating a statement about something being true will create neural connections as though we were experiencing the thing as true and were merely making a statement of fact. For instance, say you were holding a sandwich and were looking at it and feeling how it felt in your hands. Neurons would fire in your brain in the areas that process the sensory data from your fingers as well as your thoughts and attitudes about the sandwich. If you didn't have a sandwich in your hands but just imagined what it looked like and how it felt on your skin, then the same neurons would fire in your brain with the same intensity as when you were actually holding it. And in both circumstances if you affirmed, "I love sandwiches," your brain would fire in the same areas, regardless of whether you were holding a sandwich or not.'

Today, repeat out loud one of your new beliefs or, if you prefer, one of these affirmations:

- ❀ I am feeling calm and peaceful.
- ❀ I am loved.
- ❀ I am feeling better and better.
- ❀ I am creating all good things in my life.
- ❀ I am supported and loved.
- ❀ I feel lovely.
- ❀ I am happy.
- ❀ I can handle anything.
- ❀ All is well.

Start with ten affirmations, using them in the morning and in the afternoon, and then adding more if you can. 'I have found that the more times I affirm something and the more gusto I say it with, the faster the changes,' says Hamilton.

Week 3

Who's in Charge?

'It is hard to fight an enemy who has outposts in your head.' – **Sally Kempton**

One of my theories is that we cannot find our 'missing peace' because we're hiding away or putting our lives on hold while we tap dance to someone else's tune, so busy with our lists of 'shoulds' that all we can do is sink down at the end of the day, exhausted and brittle. I call it the 'boiled frog' syndrome.

Why? Well, there is a fact about frogs that isn't particularly pleasant. I don't actually want to know how anyone knows this, but the fact is that if you put a frog in a vat of water and let the water slowly heat up, the frog will become so soporific that it doesn't jump out but slowly boils to death. However, if you were to put a frog in water that was already boiling hot, it would jump out immediately.

It's the same for humans. Life can get really 'hot' and uncomfortable without us really noticing or acknowledging it. Gradually it gets worse and worse until our energy is completely drained and we no longer have the strength to jump free of our situation. Pain is usually our warning system: when we feel pain, we take action to avoid it. But if the 'water' slowly gets hot, we become lulled into a false sense of security. We get used to the heat, we begin to enjoy the heat, and then, just as it's getting a little bit too hot, we are so woozy we can't stir ourselves to action.

We can all get used to living with a constant feeling of discontent. How many times have you left behind a difficult situation – by changing jobs, leaving your partner, moving away from the neighbours from hell or simply going on holiday – only to suddenly recognize what you have been tolerating? It's only then that you look back and wonder, 'How did I ever stand it?'

But we *do* stand it, because when we're in it, we think it's normal. We don't feel like we've got a choice. We feel as if we just have to put up with it. It's a passive state. We're so soporific that it feels like only an act of God or a gargantuan effort would change things – or worse, we're going to have to be really, really brave!

Courage is a massively underrated virtue, if you ask me. When people ask me what makes my clients so special that they go on to achieve great things, I always say they're not special. (Bear with me.) Yes, my clients are talented and clever and interesting, but so what? So are many people. What sets my clients apart from the crowd is they are braver. They have the guts to leap out of the lovely warm water and go for it, to put their head above the parapet, and dare to fail – and dare to be brilliant.

In Week 3 I'm encouraging you to be brave. I know you might say that this is not exactly the best route to inner peace, but I disagree. What I'm realizing is that when we are brave, when we have courage, when we 'do the thing we think we cannot do' – we leap right into The Big Peace. When we live the life we know is right for us, or take the path that is right for us, yes, it feels scary – but ultimately it feels peaceful. It makes you feel fulfilled, on course, on the right path.

When we procrastinate, when we pretend we 'don't know' and hang around in the shallows of making do or tolerating what we don't want, THAT is what can create the most anxiety – the low-level type of anxiety, which causes us to numb ourselves with drink or crap telly and makes us feel 'itchy for more', or has us reaching for the better handbag or better house or car. But when you take the leap into making the right decisions (for you) rather than the ones that everyone says you should make, life opens up and you feel full again.

So brace yourself: in Week 3 we're going to be doing a couple of scary things. I'm going to encourage you to step out of denial and make some scary decisions about uprooting what is not working in your life. You are then going to decide who is going to be in charge of your mind. Oh yes, it's all happening in Week 3!

It's very much a process, so please don't panic or bolt on Day 16 or 17. At this point we're only doing this on paper, in theory. But it's a great exercise in discovering if you've appointed the right 'life chief'.

Big Peace Day 15: Stop Boiling Your Frog to Death

'Grant me the serenity to accept the things I cannot change, the courage to change the things I can, and the wisdom to know the difference.'
– **Reinhold Niebuhr**

Today, ask yourself: Are you a frog about to be boiled to death? How can you tell? Look at this list:

1. You wake up every morning and switch the snooze button on at least five times.
2. You tell someone about your life/situation and they react in a shocked or horrified way, and say things like 'You shouldn't have to stand for this.'
3. You daydream about your situation coming to an end by way of an act of God – a car accident, a fire or a tornado (that will whisk you off to the land of Oz, of course).
4. You sleep, watch television, drink or do drugs – a lot.
5. You avoid having conversations about your situation with 'motivated' friends, relatives or colleagues. They don't really understand what it's like and they'll just 'go on' at you.
6. You hang around with other people who are slowly boiling to death, swapping survival skills, saying things like 'It's warm in here, isn't it?' To which you reply, 'Yeah, but if you keep moving from foot to foot, it's not so bad.'
7. You blame other people – usually one particular person – for what is happening to you, and can talk about this person endlessly – how they are impossible to work for/live with, etc.

8. You feel you are powerless to change the situation.

9. You drive very fast at inappropriate moments, or sleep with inappropriate people, or put your life at risk on a weekly basis (see point 3).

10. You are dealing with niggling health problems on a daily basis, like back pain, skin problems, being overweight or becoming increasingly sluggish and lacking in energy.

Is it feeling a bit hot in here, or is that just me? It's not popular to be downbeat. 'Actually my life is crap,' would probably not go down well at your Friends Reunited reunion. But today, I want you to get out of the pan of warm water and out of denial. Write it all down.

❀ What is currently making you unhappy?

❀ Where are you betraying yourself right now?

❀ Where are you playing small in your life?

❀ What has been the lowest point in the last month? Describe that point in detail. How did it make you feel about yourself?

❀ What do you have to believe about yourself to create this situation in your life?

❀ What is the thing you are most afraid to say out loud about your life?

* What are you scared is happening to you?
* If you were run over by a bus tomorrow, what would be your greatest regret?

I know these are big questions, but this is a liberating process. Tune in for your next step tomorrow.

Big Peace Day 16: Do the Thing You Cannot Do

'Courage is the price that life extracts for granting peace.' – Amelia Earhart

Often we stay in denial and don't look at the things that are not working in our lives because we know that if we do, we may have to do something about them.

OK, I know we're only three weeks into the programme, but today I want you to make a big leap. Yesterday it was about facing up to some of the things that are keeping you stuck. Today I'm going to ask you to do something about them – on paper, at least.

Be brave.

Today, on paper only, ask yourself:
* What is the thing you think you cannot do?
* What would you do next if you were brave?

✿ If you're about to boil to death, what do you
   have to do?

Just answer the questions. You don't have to do
anything … yet.

Now just sit for 15 minutes and watch your
thought bubbles. Notice your thoughts, observe your
reaction. How does your body feel?

Big Peace Day 17: Meet Your Inner Pessimist

*'If we see light at the end of the tunnel, it's the light
of the oncoming train.'* – **Robert Lovell**

How are you feeling? That all went a bit fast – didn't
it? One second we were talking about watching our
thoughts and changing our thoughts and meditating a
bit, and the next I'm asking you to take a giant leap.

I asked you to do that because this enables you to
have that very immediate and usually quite physical
reaction of FEAR. And to observe how that feels and
what we think when we're in the fear state.

Fear is triggered in what is known as the
'reptilian' brain. It's a very ancient part of the brain
dating back to the reptiles – hence the name – and
hard-wired to react to danger or threat. Its key role
is to broadcast messages to protect us from harm.
It had a great role to play when we were cavemen

or in a situation where 'fight or flight' meant just that: lions and tigers and bears (Oh my!) are on the loose. In contemporary society, however, where social conflicts are more likely than encounters with predators, a harmless but emotionally charged situation can trigger uncontrollable fear or anger, leading to arguments and stress. We can find ourselves lying in bed worrying over some imaginary threat and left with that nameless anxiety that has nowhere to go and leaves us tearing the sheets with our teeth, wringing our hands and doing the headless chicken dance, fearful but doing nothing. Not good.

For Day 17, I want you to become fully acquainted with what happens to you when your reptilian brain is triggered, and what happens to your body when you are feeling THE FEAR – and what thoughts you think when you get THE FEAR. Awareness is everything.

Today I'd like you to personify FEAR and give it a name. I call it your Inner Pessimist and you're probably very well acquainted with him (or her) already. Always there, at every crossroads in life, hovering in the wings. You've decided to leave your career and company car behind to explore India, or you've decided to leave your diaphragm in the cupboard to try for a baby, or you've decided to leave your wife and home to discover yourself. The truth is that you're leaving the struggle behind to live a delightful life; you're leaving the warmth and safety of what you know to start something new and you're scared, but you're going to try anyway. 'Oh, you don't wanna be doing that ...' says the Inner Pessimist. 'What have I got to lose?' you ask yourself. 'Everything!' shouts your Inner Pessimist.

If only the Inner Pessimist lived in the real world. Then we could tell our Inner Pessimist to mind his or her own business. But the Inner Pessimist I'm talking about doesn't live on your street; he or she lives in your head.

When you've come out of denial, you're in a very vulnerable position. You need lots of soothing encouragement, hand-holding and acknowledgement. Your Inner Pessimist knows this, and is ready to pounce. Your Inner Pessimist will say 'I'm just being realistic.' Don't be fooled – your Inner Pessimist is ready to dismiss, negate and pour scorn on every one of your ideas and dreams.

Ten things your Inner Pessimist is mostly likely to say:

1. You're not good enough. I'd shelve this idea if I were you.
2. You're a loser. Good try, but it's best to quit while you're ahead.

3. You're really stupid! Whatever you do, don't open your mouth.
4. Really they all despise you and laugh at you behind your back. I'd stay in if I were you.
5. You're fat, your nose is huge and you're funny-looking. They would never fancy you in a month of Sundays, so don't make a fool of yourself.
6. You're talentless. Don't show anyone your work or you'll just humiliate yourself.
7. They're rich and posh and you're common and poor. Never the twain shall meet.
8. You might have hit a lucky streak but it will all go wrong soon. I wouldn't celebrate if I were you.
9. You're poor, you're stupid and you're ugly – and you're thinking about doing what?! Oh, don't make me laugh …
10. You life is terrible because you are terrible.

Many of us can live our lives thinking that our Inner Pessimist is the voice of truth because of the huge, starring role he or she plays in our head. The Inner Pessimist shouts so loudly that we don't think there's an alternative.

The good news is, there is, but we're going to find out about that tomorrow. For now, I don't want you to fight your Inner Pessimist; I simply want you to be aware of your Inner Pessimist. Learn to recognize that voice, style and script, and how you feel in your body when your Inner Pessimist is in charge.

Try this exercise:

1: Give your Inner Pessimist a name and a character. Write a description of him/her. Does he or she have dyed hair, an orange tan and a thin-lipped smile? Go to town and really flesh her or him out. How does she or he speak? In high-pitched tones, in a dull monotone or in a vicious rant?

2: You're probably very familiar with the script that your Inner Pessimist generally uses. Answer the following questions:

- ❀ What is the pessimistic script which keeps me frozen in the headlights of fear? (Be specific – write the script out in great detail.)
- ❀ How does that script serve me? (e.g. 'It allows me to torture myself so I keep myself small, which means I don't have to move out of my comfort zone, make a commitment to anything new or risk getting hurt.')
- ❀ What does it cost me? (e.g. 'I feel unbearably miserable. It costs me true peace of mind.')
- ❀ When your inner pessimist is in charge, how do you feel physically? Exhausted? Fed up? Wired? Where do you feel it in your body? (I always

get a pain between my shoulder blades and a feeling of exhaustion. I can't smile properly and my lips stick to my teeth if I try.) How do you feel and look?

That's all for today.

Big Peace Day 18: Meet Your Inner Coach

'It is better to light a candle than curse the darkness.'
– ancient Chinese proverb

I asked you to be brave on Day 16 while you wrote down the things you think you cannot do. That probably unleashed your Inner Pessimist – a personification of fear triggered in the ancient, reptilian part of our brain, which evolved to keep us safe from harm and which goes off like a bomb in our head when it perceives a threat.

Today I want you to meet your Inner Coach – the personification of love triggered in the part of the brain which I call the Big Peace place. Scientists have discovered that when we are feeling peaceful, we light up the left prefrontal lobe of the brain. This is the area of the brain that evolved later in human history – and is associated with happiness, creativity, the ability to understand right from wrong – and inner peace.

The bad news is that the way we are wired means our reptilian brain often dominates because, in evolutionary terms, it's important to be able to react to threats quickly. A state of inner peace may make us happier in the long run, but when we're being pursued by a lion it's not going to be of much help.

The structures in the primitive brain that trigger the flight or fight response are virtually automatic, while the ability to let go of fear and find a place of inner peace and calm is a much rarer brain state. And one we need to practise.

So today, let's create a new character to practise with. Let's call this character your Inner Coach. The Big Peace personified. The one who will champion your dreams and tell you to have faith when all seems dark, the one who will send help when the going gets tough – and a very peaceful presence to invite into your life.

Ten things your Inner Coach is likely to say:

1. You don't have to do anything to be loved.
2. You are smart, beautiful and funny.
3. Whatever happens, no matter how this turns out, you're going to be fine.
4. Oh, stop taking it all so seriously. In 12 months from now you won't even be able to remember what you were worrying about. Smile.

5. You have many gifts – when are you going to start using them?
6. Everyone doubts themselves, it's normal. Have faith. You're going to be OK.
7. What are you learning here?
8. Hold my hand, take a deep breath and now stop.
9. You don't have to do anything to be accepted. Just be who you are.
10. When are you going to start having some fun?

The Inner Coach speaks from a different place than your Inner Pessimist. While your Inner Pessimist speaks in your head, motivated by fear – a rattling, obsessive drone that takes you round and round in circles, going nowhere – your Inner Coach speaks through your body, not through your thoughts. Your Inner Coach talks through your gut instinct, your feelings and your intuition. You cannot justify the messages of your Inner Coach through logic. You know you've heard your Inner Coach when you hear yourself saying: 'It's just a feeling I've got' or 'My gut feeling is telling me something.'

Ten ways to tell when your Inner Coach is speaking to you:

1. Your decision 'feels' right.
2. You 'just know' that this is the right path.

3. You are very clear about what it is you want.
4. You feel relaxed and happy about your decision.
5. You feel like you're in 'the flow'. Coincidences start happening. 'You'll never believe it …' is your favourite phrase.
6. You feel a flicker of excitement in your stomach.
7. You trust your inklings and intuition even though you have no evidence to back them up.
8. Even though life doesn't look like it's going in the right direction, you know it is.
9. You find yourself inspired with ideas more often than before.
10. You begin to trust your decisions.

Today, I want you to get to know your Inner Coach so you have a clear picture or vision of what it feels like when you're communicating with each other. Try this exercise:

1: Imagine you've invited your Inner Coach for tea and biscuits. What does he or she look like? Angel wings, dressed in white? Wearing jeans? How does your Inner Coach speak? How do you know that he or she is speaking? How do you feel in your body when you hear the words?
2: You're probably not that familiar with your Inner Coach's script. The Inner Pessimist is such a bully

that your Inner Coach usually gets drowned out. If your Inner Coach were to speak, what words would you hear? How do you know your Inner Coach is speaking to you?

❀ When you're afraid – what does your Inner Coach say? (Be specific – write the script out in great detail.)

❀ When you feel you're not good enough, what does your Inner Coach say?

❀ When you feel ugly, what does your Inner Coach say?

❀ When you feel sad, what does your Inner Coach say?

❀ When you're exhausted, what does your Inner Coach say?

❀ What script would you have to hear to create the life you really want? (Write this script in great detail.)

❀ How do you feel in your body when you know that you are listening to your Inner Coach? (I feel calm, expansive, sure, forgiving, more loving, my shoulders drop five inches, I laugh, I smile, I'm more curious.) What do you feel like?

Big Peace Day 19: Who's in Charge?

'We can never obtain peace in the outer world until we make peace with ourselves.' – Dalai Lama

OK, in the past couple of days we've met your Inner Pessimist and Inner Coach. The last thing we want to happen is to have these two characters at war with each other – it's not very peaceful. We need them to work together. Your Inner Pessimist may seem like the baddie but, in fact, often has useful stuff to say.

The trick is appointing your Inner Coach as the one in charge. Your Inner Coach needs to be the head gardener in the garden of your mind, otherwise your landscape is going to look very gloomy indeed – you will be growing negative pathways in your brain versus lovely, blossoming, peaceful pathways.

Today we're going to bring your Inner Pessimist and Inner Coach together into the same room, in an exercise that I've found to be incredibly powerful when working with my clients.

Today, I want you to try this visualization.

Imagine your Inner Pessimist as a little boy or girl – a child of around six to eight years old. I want you to imagine that you are seeing the world and life through this six-year-old's eyes. What is your Inner Pessimist afraid of?

Rather than fighting with, chastising or sending this child to his or her room, I want you to imagine your Inner Coach comforting your little Inner Pessimist child. I want you to give that little child the comfort and love and encouragement he or she needs to stop feeling afraid and feel safe again.

My Inner Coach is very good at putting a blanket around my little Inner Pessimist's shoulders and telling him all the things he needs to hear. My Inner Coach is also really good at listening. I want you to imagine you can hear the scared ramblings of a little child, and imagine your Inner Coach comforting that child. What does your Inner Coach say? How is it said? How can this scared little child in your head be comforted?

I know this sounds like I'm trying to turn you barmy, but I have found this to be one of the most powerful exercises I have worked with.

Your Inner Pessimist is scared. Scared witless. If you're going to 'do the thing you cannot do', it's much easier to calm your Inner Pessimist down first. In my case this means I stop ignoring him. So stop putting your fingers in your ears and start being reassuring. You'll be amazed at what happens when you do. Get your Inner Coach to look your little Inner Pessimist right in the eye and offer plenty of hugs and comfort until your Inner Pessimist stops being afraid.

This visualization works because when you allow your Inner Coach to comfort your Inner Pessimist, you are lighting up the prefrontal lobes of your brain and showing compassion and love for yourself. According to medical psychologists, it's physiologically *impossible* for your mind to be scared while at the same time generating love and compassion.

So try this visualization today.

Big Peace Day 20: Hypnotize Your Inner Pessimist

'He was of those who hypnotize themselves, who glow with self-creation, who flower and bloom without pollen.' – Gilbert Parker

A couple of years ago I met a wonderful hypnotherapist called Georgia Foster, author of *The Drink-Less Mind*, *The Weight-Less Mind* and *The 4 Secrets of Amazing Sex*.

When she explained to me how hypnotherapy worked (I was always a bit wary before – I'd conjured up pictures of swinging watches and eating onions), I felt like I'd found the missing piece (peace?). I went on to create a Big Peace hypnotherapy CD with Georgia, and now I listen to it every day. Not because I particularly like the sound of my own voice, but because it helps enormously in reprogramming my old ways of thinking – and it helps me keep the fear and my Inner Pessimist at bay.

How? The deeper part of the mind, the unconscious mind, is where all of our emotional habits are stored. This part of the mind learns very quickly how to respond to life, whether positively or negatively. It's like a library that provides you references for how to deal with whatever comes your way. If you think the glass is always half empty rather than half full, this is simply because your mind *believes* it to be true – but it's not the truth. It's simply a learned behaviour.

'This negative thinking is driven by a fearful voice which you call the Inner Pessimist, Suzy,' says Georgia.

'This part plays havoc with any desires to feel better because it thinks that being negative prepares you for bad things that might happen. This creates physical anxieties and fears about the future that hold you back from feeling calm, confident and trusting in your life.

'It may seem bizarre, but the mind doesn't know the difference between positive or negative. It doesn't understand that being at peace is better than feeling anxious. It doesn't know that feeling safe is better for you than feeling scared. The mind is like a library and simply through life experiences your mind will use past experiences as your response, whether you consciously want to or not!

'If you deal with life by negative thinking, even though these experiences are not supporting you, your mind will assume this is the correct response because this is the only information your mind has.

'The best way to start to feel the energy of your Inner Coach is to practise what it feels like to be present in your daily life. If you have enough time to be negative, then you have enough time to be positive and the more you tune in to the voice of your Inner Coach, the more you will be free to think good thoughts which will create great outcomes in your life.

'Your inner library, at present, represents every memory and some of them may be holding you back. In order for you to build a new library that is stronger than your past habit, you need repetition, such as hypnosis. The only way to combat old out-of-date information is to build your new library with the opposite information. The more you practise, the stronger it will become. The repetition is extremely important.'

I'll let Georgia set the homework today. 'A great way to start to locate your Inner Coach is with the following exercise,' she says.

'We rarely give ourselves adequate time to relax and recharge. Schedule relaxation time for at least 20 mindful minutes each day to spend with your Inner Coach. The more you schedule this 'me' time into your life, the better you will cope with the challenges of day-to-day life and improve your emotional well-being.'

Your mind knows how to relax and find peace, it just needs the space, time and, most importantly, the practice. The more you do this mind exercise, the more it will become a habit.

Find somewhere to lie down or sit comfortably where you know you will be warm and safe. As you close your eyes, start to become aware of your breathing. Tension and negative thinking create shallow breathing, so this is a great way to start to train your mind and body to feel good and think positive thoughts. Take a big deep breath in and hold for five seconds, then release and count for five. Do this three times. This will start to calm you down.

Now imagine a situation in your life where
you want to be more healthy, positive and life-
affirming. See yourself coping better and feeling
better. If any Inner Pessimist thoughts or feelings
creep in, release them on the out-breath, then
say to yourself with the voice of your Inner Coach
on the next in-breath, 'I am feeling calm and
confident.'

As Georgia says, 'If there are any situations in your life where you feel unsafe and anxious, imagine seeing yourself in the experience coping better and feeling calm and safe. The more you practise this positive exercise of how you want to think and feel, the more your mind thinks it is how you truly are meant to live your life.'

Big Peace Day 21: Tune In to Big Peace Radio

'My therapist told me the way to achieve true inner peace is to finish what I start. So far today, I have finished two bags of M&Ms and a chocolate cake. I feel better already.' – **Dave Barry**

It's been a big week, so I just want to finish on a reminder to be aware and keep observing rather than being in amongst your thoughts. Start to notice when you are wolfing down a meal without tasting it. Start noticing when you are driving and arrive at your destination and think, 'How did I get here?' Notice when your shoulders are round your ears, and let them drop.

Mostly we exist on autopilot – our busy minds behaving like what some call 'the chattering monkey' (mine feels like a drunken one!), so full of thoughts that we become completely unaware of the present moment.

Today, notice when you zone out and bring yourself back to observing your inner dialogue. What is your Inner Pessimist ranting about today? Shrink him or her into a child and see if you can summon your Inner Coach to the rescue. Tune in to his or her soothing words and reassurance. Tune in to Big Peace radio. Tune in as often as you can today.

Week 4

What's Your Story?

'And the day came when the risk to remain tight in a bud was more painful than the risk it took to blossom.' – **Anais Nin**

Recently, I've been attempting to write a little bit of fiction. I have always loved reading stories, and am now enjoying writing them.

I was inspired by a screenwriting course I attended in Cornwall led by Hollywood guru Blake Snyder, author of *Save the Cat! The Only Book on Screenwriting You'll Ever Need*.

I just wanted to share this post on Blake's blog (www.blakesnyder.com): 'All stories are about transformation. All stories are the caterpillar turning into a butterfly in some sense. All stories require a death and rebirth to make that painful and glorious process happen.

'And it occurs in movies ... and in life.

'We transform every day, reawaken to new concepts about the world around us, overcome conflict, and triumph over death ... only to start again each morning.

'It's why stories that follow this pattern resonate. Because each day is a transformation machine and so are our lives.'

In Week 4, I'd like you to try out the Big Peace Transformation Machine – where we're going to use techniques, questions and tools to transform some of the most peace-robbing stories and mindsets that my clients (and I) struggle with.

Our stories are potent combinations of beliefs and unmet needs we tell ourselves every day in the voice of our Inner Pessimist (or Inner Coach, if we're lucky). For example, my favourite story used to be 'poor, brave me'. I was the world's favourite martyr. I did everything for everyone else – I was a giving friend, a dutiful daughter, and a wife who supported her husband emotionally (and financially, for a while). And how was I? 'Fine, if a little bit tired/ stressed/worn out', I'd say with a little sigh.

Playing the happy helper was how I'd got love and attention as a child. At some point I'd made the decision that love wasn't unconditional and I would have to do a, b and c to be loved.

I'd clean the house for my parents; I was the good one who wouldn't stay out late because I didn't want my parents to worry; I was the sweet, giving one of the family. I got lavished with praise, love and attention. It was glorious. I was loved by almost everyone. Everyone would say how lovely I was. No one could ever criticize me or say anything bad about me because I was doing everything 'right', I was being there for everyone, was 'sweet and kind' and 'only trying to help'. It got me love and approval.

However, 30 years on it wasn't working for me any more. I was twitchy with resentment. I was constantly screening my answering machine because friends were always ringing me to dump their problems on me. 'No one ever listens to me,' I'd sigh. I resented my husband for having the freedom and money to go off and follow his dreams even though I couldn't follow mine; but I'd never say anything, I'd just stew inwardly. 'You go on, darling, and be happy. I'll just sit here and be miserable.' I know: nothing so revolting as the smell of burning martyr, is there?

I'd find myself working all the hours because I didn't want to say 'No' to my bosses. I wanted everyone to like me and think I was incredibly hard working and dynamic. Predictably, I began to lose my energy. I started to use stimulants such as coffee and cigarettes to help me get through the days, as

73

I was constantly exhausted. Which meant I got to 'sigh' all the more and, yes, I still got to be a martyr. But eventually, I was fed up with it. It was costing me big time – my health and my sanity.

I had to find a new way of thinking and I had to create a new story and way to behave. It's not easy and it does make you feel incredibly vulnerable. We have created these stories to protect ourselves from hurt and to get our needs met, so like a hero of a story, we must be brave and overcome the obstacles if we want our old ways of operating to 'die' and a new way of being to be 'born'.

In the next few days, I want to explore some of the core stories I hear my clients tell me and see if we can't uproot them and find a more life-affirming Big Peace story instead. We're going to work through a 7-step transformation process that I use when working with my clients – brilliant for challenging stubborn mindsets and stories and for creating more peace in our lives.

Obviously, every day this week won't be relevant to you. If you don't resonate with any particular day this week, spend 15 minutes every day observing your thought bubbles instead. However, if you recognize one of the mindsets, do try to work through the step-by-step transformation process.

Let's free a few butterflies.

Big Peace Day 22: The Big Peace Transformation Machine

'Life begins at the end of your comfort zone.'
– Neale Donald Walsch

Today, let's work through the Big Peace transformation process. When you've been telling yourself a story for most of your life, it doesn't change overnight. There are still times I find myself 'sighing' and saying 'Yes' when I mean 'No,' which leads to old peace-robbing behaviours of drinking too much coffee or wine to numb the pain.

But nowadays, I do catch myself quicker. Rather than going through weeks or months of martyrdom, I only do it for a day or less now. Sometimes I even manage to catch myself in the moment. And for me, it's often a moment-by-moment practice, being aware of my old thoughts and replacing them so I can then do something differently.

THE 7-STEP TRANSFORMATION MACHINE
Step 1: Coming Out of the Closet
It's difficult to change thoughts and behaviours if you're in denial. If you don't think you are a martyr, then you probably won't want to change your story.

If you don't think you have a 'story', read this
week's tasks and see if you resonate with any of
them.

Step 2: What Does It Give You?

In Step 2, we question how this story benefits your
life. Does it protect you from disappointment? Get
you approval? Respect? Love? What needs does this
story fulfil for you?

Step 3: What Does It Cost You?

Most people won't even think about questioning their
story if the costs don't outweigh the benefits. But
usually at some point in our lives, the story we tell
ourselves about life actually starts to become painful
or costs us energy or loses us the very thing we're
trying to get – be it a healthy relationship or inner
peace.

Step 4: What Do You Do When You're in Story
Mode?

Here you make a list of symptoms of what you do
when you're doing the martyr thing – like sighing a
lot or washing the kitchen floor at 4 a.m. The more
ways you have of jolting your awareness, the
better.

Step 5: Transforming the Old Story to a Big Peace Story

Once you are aware of what you *don't* want, you can make the leap to changing your mindset or story to one that will get you what you *do* want – love, respect, peace. We do this by creating a new thought, belief or story to tell. For instance, what if you chose to believe that people love you for who you are rather than what you do for them? In Step 5, we ask the simple question 'What would you have to believe to feel at peace in this situation?'

Step 6: Creating a Big Peace Thought Leap

I have found it incredibly useful to have a phrase or word that I can use in the moment to help me make the leap from my old story to my new one. My Big Peace thought leap is: From 'poor me' to 'lucky me'.

It works every time.

Step 7: Creating a Big Peace Action Plan

In Step 7 you make a list of all the things you could do differently if you could come from your Big Peace mindset.

Today, ask yourself, What story do you think you tell yourself? Is yours a tragedy? High drama? Triumph over adversity? A comedy? We'll work on the specifics in the next few days.

Big Peace Day 23: Transforming the Martyr (Sigh)

'Although prepared for martyrdom, I prefer that it be postponed.' – Winston Churchill

Today we're going to look at transforming the 'martyrdom' story by using the 7-step transformation process.

Step 1: Coming Out of the Closet

Are you a martyr? Are you the giving friend, the dutiful son or daughter, the hard-working employee putting in the extra hours, the spouse who tirelessly supports your partner, the parent who always puts the kids first? Are you a really good egg, reliable, kind and always there for everyone?

Do you find yourself feeling resentful, constantly exhausted and sighing a lot? You know you've lost your mojo but you're so busy sorting out everyone else, you haven't got the energy to find it again.

If this list rings a few bells, you may be playing the martyr in your life:

❀ You do everything for everyone else – while quietly (and sometimes not so quietly) resenting it.

❧ If someone asked you what you wanted or what you needed at any given time in the day, you wouldn't have a clue – but you'd know what your partner/children/parents did.

❧ You find yourself sighing a lot.

❧ You say things like, 'Don't worry about me, I'll just stay in and do that for you (sigh).'

❧ You feel constantly exhausted.

Score 3 or more? Time to take action.

Step 2: What Does It Give You?

The martyrdom mindset often gets set up in childhood. Early on we discover that we get approval for being the 'giving', 'good' person. It's a common trap, especially for women but also for plenty of men out there. Many of us are brought up on the belief system that we must look after others before ourselves. The martyrdom story is a seductive one because it works very well – we do get approval, love and attention for being seen as such a 'good' person. On the surface, all this 'helping' might look as if we're being 'self-less', but in fact, often we're just getting our own emotional needs met – in an unhealthy way. Beneath our quiet martyrdom lies a bed of our own seething unmet needs – to be loved, to be needed, to be approved of and to feel secure. And beneath those unmet needs lie beliefs we learned in childhood that we are not good enough/ love is conditional/we must do a + b + c to be loved. So answer the question: What am I hoping to get from all my giving? Be specific. Is it so you can feel appreciated, loved, needed so they (partner/parents/ children) won't leave?

Step 3: What Does It Cost You?

Giving time and energy to our family, loved ones or jobs is not a bad thing, but if it's at the expense at ourselves, I would suggest that it's not entirely healthy, either. And the balance can be so easily tipped if you have children, or your parents fall ill, or your work becomes more demanding – you may find that you can't cope any more. You are trying to give, give, give but your tank is empty and so your health and life begin to suffer. Let's see if we can transform this story.

Step 4: What Do You Do When You're in Story Mode?

Specifically, write a list of all the things that you do when you're in martyr-mode – saying 'Yes' to looking after your friend's children, having the whole family for Christmas dinner, spending every night working in the office 'til 9.

Step 5: Transforming the Old Story to a Big Peace Story

How would your life change if any of the following statements were true? Explore your answers by writing about each one.

- ❀ I am enough.
- ❀ I am loved for who I am, not for what I do or give to others.

Describe how you would feel if this were true? What would you do differently? How would you behave in social situations, at work, with your friends, with your partner? What parts of your life would change?

Step 6: Creating a Big Peace Thought Leap

From 'Love is conditional' to 'I am loved.'

Step 7: Creating a Big Peace Action Plan

- ❀ Create an evidence-building project. Rather than trying to get everyone to appreciate/like/ approve of you by doing everything for them or constantly saying 'Yes' at the expense of your own needs, set up a 'needs fulfilment exercise' with two of your closest friends.
- ❀ Ask your chosen friends to tell you one thing that they love/appreciate/approve of about you every day for the next few weeks. You could get them to email you/leave a message on your

answerphone or even send you a daily postcard.
Set it up formally, with an agreement that you
all sign. This is a very powerful exercise. A
martyr often finds it very uncomfortable to
receive from other people. Grit your teeth and
allow yourself to be supported – feel what that
feels like. It may make you quite emotional,
as receiving from others can make you feel
very vulnerable. Often we give, give, give and
sort everyone else out because it means we're
in control. Throughout this evidence-building
project, you are learning that it is possible to
trust and receive from others and that they will
be there for you.

❀ Practise saying 'No!' Create ten new ways of
saying 'No' but still getting approved of. You
can even use stock phrases such as, 'I can't
help you but I know a man who can.'

❀ Constantly ask yourself: What do I want and
need here? Martyrs are often completely out of
touch with their own needs and wants, so ask
yourself this question at every decision point.

❀ Do something just for you once a day. Treat
yourself to time off, a treat or indulgence
of some type. Start to get comfortable with
putting yourself first.

Big Peace Day 24: Transforming the Perfectionist

'Perfectionism is not a quest for the best. It is a pursuit of the worst in ourselves, the part that tells us that nothing we do will ever be good enough – that we should try again.' – Julia Cameron, *The Artist's Way*

Today, we're going to look at transforming the 'perfectionist' story as we work through the 7-step transformation process.

Step 1: Coming Out of the Closet
Are you a perfectionist?

Perfectionism is one of the most common drivers in my clients. Do any of these ring true for you?

* No matter how well you do it, it's never quite right.
* You constantly compare yourself to others and find yourself lacking.
* You're the boss who has to oversee every last detail, or the parent who won't let anyone look after the children because of your high standards.
* You're most likely to say: 'You're doing it wrong. Give it to me.'
* You work 18 hours a day, 7 days a week at work/ for the family. You're never able to take time off unless you're ill.

Step 2: What Does It Give You?

A perfectionist believes that if he can achieve
perfection, he will be loved and approved of.
Perfectionism is another 'survival mechanism' we learn
in childhood. As a child, you built a belief system that
said you weren't good enough/clever enough/enough
just as you are. Scratch any perfectionist and you'll
usually find a five-year-old who has decided that to be
loved they must attain perfection.

Step 3: What Does It Cost You?

Perfectionism is a glorious way of setting yourself
up to fail in spectacular style. It is a way to reaffirm
constantly to yourself that 'you're no good'/not up
to the mark/are failing every single day of your life'.
Perfectionism is simply a way of constantly trying
to prove to the world that you are good enough. It
is exhausting and self-defeating, because generally
no matter how hard you try you will always find
yourself lacking.

Step 4: What Do You Do When You're in Story Mode?

Perfectionists set themselves an impossible task.
Their standards are so high that they never can
relax and give themselves a pat on the back. There
is always, always something better they could have

done. The perfectionist will focus on that tiny detail that wasn't quite right rather on the massive, amazing event/meal/report that they have just completed.

Step 5: Transforming the Old Story to a Big Peace Story

What new story can you tell yourself? Imagine if the following statements were true: how would your life change? Explore your answers by writing about each one.

❀ I am loved unconditionally.

❀ I'm not perfect and I am loved.

❀ I'm not perfect but I'm fabulous.

Step 6: Creating a Big Peace Thought Leap

From 'It has to be right' to 'Everything will be OK, it's all working out perfectly.'

Step 7: Creating a Big Peace Action Plan

OK, there is a lot of list-writing on this one.

❀ List your 'imperfections'. Ask yourself why people love and like you even with these imperfections, or why, even if they are irritated by your 'imperfections', they still seem to love you anyway?

❀ Create an evidence wall or simply write a list of all the things you observe today that are wonderful despite being imperfect. Today write down the reasons why imperfection can often be someone's greatest attraction. Think of your friends and loved ones and think of three of their best 'imperfections' – why do you love them, and does their 'imperfection' make you love them any less?

Big Peace Day 25: Transforming the Worrier

'I will not die an unlived life. I will not live in fear of falling or catching fire. I choose to inhabit my days, to allow my living to open me, to make me less afraid, more accessible, to loosen my heart until it becomes a wing, a torch, a promise. I choose to risk my significance; to live so that which comes to me as seed goes to the next as blossom and that which comes to me as blossom, goes on as fruit'

– Dawna Markova

Today, we're going to work with the worriers out there. I've got quite a lot to say about this one because it's one of my personal favourites. I always remember when my coach asked me: What if worrying was optional?

Worrying? Optional? Well, if only that were true. I suppose it might be true for some people but not me.

Sigh. I'm just a worrier. I worry about everything. Sigh. I constantly worry about what people think, I worry about what might happen, I worry about what might not happen. That's just the way I am. Sigh. You can't get through life without worrying – can you?

Is this you?

Step 1: Coming Out of the Closet
Are you a worrier?

❀ You can get exhausted by the nameless anxiety that tends to dog you, and you see threat and danger everywhere.

❀ Sometimes you feel like the sky is about to fall in.

❀ You are constantly thinking 'Am I doing this right? What's the right way? Oh, my God, what if I get this wrong?'

❀ You find it hard to trust that everything really will be OK.

❀ You worry about the good stuff, too. If you won the lottery, you'd worry about what you'd do with the money.

Step 2: What Does It Give You?
You manage your anxiety by worrying because you think it will protect you somehow. If you imagine the worst, then you are prepared. Worrying is also

the way you protect yourself from disappointment. If you worry about something, then you won't be so disappointed if it doesn't happen.

Step 3: What Does It Cost You?

You don't feel joy all that often! You feel battered down by life and you feel like you're constantly scanning the world for threats – and because what you focus on expands, you find more and more that threatens your life and survival. You feel constantly anxious, which can spiral quite easily into depression.

Step 4: What Do You Do When You're in Story Mode?

Write a list of ten symptoms/actions that suggest that you're in the midst of a worry fest. For example: you stand and eat at the fridge, you clean your kitchen floor obsessively (I wish I had that response to anxiety), you pick your nose.

Step 5: Transforming the Old Story to a Big Peace Story

How would your life change if any of the following statements were true? Explore your answers by writing about each one.

❀ I trust that I handle most things that are thrown at me.
❀ Whatever happens, I'll find the right support to get me through whatever life throws at me.
❀ I do the best I can with what is happening right now.
❀ I trust myself.

Step 6: Creating a Big Peace Thought Leap
From 'I'm worried' to 'I'm safe.'

From 'Everything's going to go wrong' to 'All will be well.'

Step 7: Creating a Big Peace Action Plan
❀ Learn to trust your own instincts more. Get in touch with what you truly know to be so – in your gut and your heart, as well as your head.
❀ At every decision point, ask yourself: If I trusted myself and my own instincts right now, what would I do or say? Make yourself your own expert on your life.
❀ Write a list or create an evidence wall of how you have managed crisis in the past.
❀ List all the reasons you can trust yourself.

Big Peace Day 26: Transforming Mr (or Ms) Right

'You only live once, but if you do it right, once is enough.' – Mae West

Today, let's transform Mr or Ms Right.

Step 1: Coming Out of the Closet
Is this you?
- ❀ You say: 'Am I right or am I right?'
- ❀ You always need to be right and really do think you are right.
- ❀ Your whole identity is wrapped up with being right.
- ❀ If someone challenges your opinion, you have a physical reaction – you get a rush of adrenalin, you come out fighting. Those who love you groan inwardly.
- ❀ You have a brilliant armoury of one-line put-downs.

Step 2: What Does It Give You?
There are big pay-offs for being right: you get to feel superior; you get to feel big and clever; you get to nod triumphantly; you get to smile winningly; you get to win. And that has to be a good thing – right?

'Being right' is a great mindset to work within. You can find lots of proof – facts, data and evidence – that almost everyone else is wrong. Most of the time. You've set up 'being right' as a way of gaining people's approval. By 'winning' an argument, you are competing for people's respect.

Step 3: What Does It Cost You?

Does being right make you feel peaceful? Well, maybe. But only when you're right. It gets you spending time and energy trying to prove to people how wrong they are, and how right you are. Needing to be right puts you under constant threat, in case someone 'proves' you wrong. Your identity becomes tied up in having to be right. Your sense of value and whether or not you are respected and liked or loved is tied up to whether you can persuade people that you are right.

Step 4: What Do You Do When You're in Story Mode?

Are you constantly trying to change others' opinions? Do you attack, belittle, manipulate in order to keep your position of 'rightness'? What do you do, for example, when someone disagrees with you and tells you why you're wrong? List the behaviours that you find yourself indulging in.

Step 5: Transforming the Old Story to a Big Peace Story

How would your life change if any of the following statements were true? Explore your answers by writing about each one.

❀ I am respected when I'm right *and* when I'm wrong.
❀ I am respected for being a good listener.
❀ What if everyone was right because they believed they were?

Step 6: Creating a Big Peace Thought Leap

From 'I'm right' to 'I'm loved whether I'm right or wrong.'

From 'I'm right' to 'I believe I'm right, and others believe they're right, so we're all right.'

From 'I'm right' to 'That's an interesting opinion, tell me more.'

Step 7: Creating a Big Peace Action Plan

Really listen to what other people say, and reflect back what you're hearing rather than trying to prove that they are wrong. 'Ah, so you believe that there are men on Mars? Tell me more.' It doesn't mean that you have to start agreeing with everyone, rather that you just accept that others have a different opinion to you. How would you make the leap from a mindset of right/wrong to one of curious enquiry?

Big Peace Day 27: Transforming the Flake

'It is better to be hated for what you are, than to be loved for something you are not.' – André Gide

Today, let's transform the flakey story!

Step 1: Coming Out of the Closet
Is this you?
- ❀ You are constantly late but always charmingly apologetic.
- ❀ You've never been out of debt.
- ❀ Your relationships are in constant upheaval.
- ❀ You can never find your mobile phone/keys/child.
- ❀ Your favourite phrase is: 'Oh, you know what I'm like'?

Step 2: What Does It Give You?
You don't have to take responsibility for your own life because you get looked after by others and get lots of attention. You are generally loved by others because you don't threaten them. People love to hear your 'disaster stories' because it makes them feel better about their own lives. You feel safe and loved and don't have to leave your comfort zone. You believe that deep down you're not talented enough or good enough to get what you want OR you believe

that you are, but that if you shine, then people will attack you for it. It's easier to stay in the shadows.

Step 3: What Does It Cost You?

Does it make you feel peaceful? Is your life in constant crisis – especially if you don't have your usual team in place to rescue you? If you want to live comfortably, you have to hook up with someone wealthy (parents or partner is usual), as your current mindset won't allow you to forge a good life on your own.

Step 4: What Do You Do When You're in Story Mode?

Giggle inappropriately, run off, give up, never complete a project, cry.

Step 5: Transforming the Old Story to a Big Peace Story

How would your life change if any of the following statements were true? Explore your answers by writing about each one.

- ❀ I can shine and people won't attack me.
- ❀ I trust myself to take responsibility for my life.
- ❀ I can calmly create what I want in my life.

Step 6: Creating a Big Peace Thought Leap

From 'I can't do this' to 'I can do it.'

From 'I'm incapable' to 'When I focus I can achieve anything.'

Step 7: Creating a Big Peace Action Plan
* ❈ Stop pretending to be hopeless. Stop hiding your talents and start taking yourself seriously.
* ❈ Look at expanding your social group so you can try out a new mode of operating – and be your most brilliant, capable self.
* ❈ Start building new evidence to prove to yourself that you can do anything you want to.

Big Peace Day 28: Transforming the Drama Queen

'We do not need magic to transform our world.'
– J K Rowling

Today, let's work with the drama queen.

Step 1: Coming Out of the Closet
Is this you?
* ❈ Your life is a constant whirl of dramatic scenes.
* ❈ Your favourite phrase is, 'You'll never guess what happened to me today.'
* ❈ You like an audience.
* ❈ Someone always says or does something that offends you.

❄ It's never your fault.

Step 2: What Does It Give You?
You get to be the centre of attention. Even if you're not there, people are talking about you. You get a lot of energy from constantly living in a high-drama atmosphere. You are compensating for a belief that you are nothing, nobody or invisible unless you're out there, centre stage, seen.

Step 3: What Does It Cost You?
Does being a drama queen make you feel peaceful? Not often. You never seem to be able to find any peace. The only 'peace' you know is in the drama. You long to simply be loved and love someone back without the turmoil.

Step 4: What Do You Do When You're in Story Mode?
You flounce, you slap, you argue with others loudly, you shout, you pout.

Step 5: Transforming the Old Story to a Big Peace Story
How would your life change if any of the following statements were true? Explore your answers by writing about each one.

❀ I am loved and I am heard when I talk calmly.
❀ I am loved.
❀ I am heard.
❀ I am seen.

Step 6: Creating a Big Peace Thought Leap
From 'I need to be noticed' to 'I am honoured, respected and loved when I am my wisest self.'

Step 7: Creating a Big Peace Action Plan
Set up a formal time to be 'listened to' by friends, a coach or a therapist about something other than a drama. Set ground rules – you don't want to be 'fixed', you just want to be heard, noticed and validated. Start building evidence that you have value and can garner respect and approval by just being yourself.

Week 5

What Do You Want?

'Too often, we decide to follow a path that is not really our own, one that others have set for us. We forget that, whichever way we go, the price is the same: in both cases we will pass through both difficult and happy moments. But when we are living our dream, the difficulties we encounter make sense.'
– Paulo Coelho

This week we're going to be working out what you really want in life, what makes you happy and what you value most – that's all! The Big Peace is about changing our thinking but it can also be about changing course in life so that our own internal emotional compass is pointing in the right direction. Sometimes we get blown off course by 'falling into' a career or a relationship and staying longer than we should.

This week we're going to be looking at ways to set sail again, to plot a new course.

One of your own making. Week 5 is not about conforming; it's about living life as you see fit and no longer doing things because you think you ought/must/should.

Imagine living a life where you do things because you want to do them. Imagine a life where you no longer have to do things to please anyone else, to gain their approval; you simply have to gain your own approval and please yourself.

This all sounds fine and dandy, but how do you know what's right for you? Most of us grew up living our lives by everyone else's rules, playing the roles that society demanded in order to be 'happy'. We got exams results, the career, the car and the house, and now can't understand why we're not happy. We did all the 'right' things, living by all the 'right' rules, so why are we desperately resentful and exhausted?

To live a congruent life, we have to start living by our own rules and rediscovering what we want for ourselves, instead of what we're told we should want. It's creating our own new rulebook, which works for us.

What do you stand for? What's really important to you? This week is about finding purpose and fulfilment, and establishing what makes you feel good and why.

Big Peace Day 29: Enjoy Yourself

'Wind in the hair, lead in the pencil!' – **Jack Nicholson as Garrett Breedlove in *Terms of Endearment***

The last few weeks have been a bit full on, with all that digging up of the past. So today, I want you to 'reward' yourself and do something you enjoy. Be specific – write a list of ten things you would love to do with a spare hour. What activities do you use to switch off, chill out?

Now choose one on your list and do it. I'll explain more of the theory in a few days' time. For now, just go and enjoy yourself.

Big Peace Day 30: The Costs of Pleasure Seeking

'I can't get no satisfaction.' – **The Rolling Stones**

Yesterday, you were having some fun. How did it feel? Did it make you feel great all day, did you feel satisfied, gratified? At one with the world? Yes or no?

Today I want us to explore your relationship with pleasure in your life.

Pleasure is often short-lived, enjoyable, fun – and there's nothing wrong with that. However, when we find ourselves chasing only pleasure, we can get stuck on that treadmill in search of the next quick-fix high, and it can get unhealthily addictive.

Our brain chemistry doesn't help. Pleasure seeking involves two ancient regions of the brain: the amygdala and the nucleus accumbens. These communicate using the chemical dopamine to form the brain's reward system. Pleasure seeking triggers the production of dopamine, which keeps you coming back for more.

Working from yesterday's list of things you reward yourself with, which ones give you that quick-fix 'pleasurable' buzz? What makes you feel good instantly but leaves you wanting more? What role does pleasure play in your life? Is it something that enhances your life, makes you feel alive, or is it compensation for being somewhat at odds with your life? Are you desperately reaching out for fun/fun/ fun, drinking too much, overshopping, taking drugs to numb your feelings or give you a fix to make you feel better about your life?

One last question: what positive and negative effects does your pleasure seeking have on your life? Do you motivate yourself with a reward system? Treat yourself with a glass of wine at the end of the day? Does that glass spill over to a half bottle, or even a whole one? What effect does that have on your energy levels and health? If shopping is your greatest source of pleasure and you reward yourself after a week at work with a shopping spree, are you left in debt?

Is your pleasure seeking enhancing your life or ruining it?

Big Peace Day 31: Find Your Flow

Tutor: What does it feel like when you're dancing?
Billy: Don't know. Sorta feels good. Sorta stiff and that, but once I get going ... then I like, forget everything. And ... sorta disappear. Sorta disappear. Like I feel a change in my whole body. And I've got this fire in my body. I'm just there. Flyin' like a bird. Like electricity. Yeah, like electricity. – Billy Elliot

Yesterday we were examining our relationship with pleasure. Today I want to talk about life satisfaction.

Mihaly Csikszentmihalyi, a psychologist from the University of Chicago, studied thousands of people for more than 30 years to discover what makes our lives meaningful and satisfying. From his research he wrote a book called *Flow*. Flow is what he describes as being involved in an activity which gives us a narrowing of attention, a sense of being absorbed and a feeling of transcendence.

The great news is that any activity can lead to flow – playing a game, listening to music, writing a novel, etc. And, in spite of the huge differences in the activities themselves, those who've experienced it – from meditating Koreans to motorcycle-gang members, chess players to sculptors to assembly-line workers – describe the psychological components of gratification in notably similar ways:

- ❀ Focusing on a task is challenging and requires skill.
- ❀ You have to concentrate.
- ❀ There are clear goals.
- ❀ You get immediate feedback.
- ❀ You have deep effortless involvement.
- ❀ There is a sense of control.
- ❀ Your sense of self vanishes.
- ❀ Time stops.

Today I'd like you to consider what gives you a sense of 'flow' in your life. What makes time disappear, what challenges you and requires skill?

You may know immediately the things that give you that feeling of flow. How often do you spend doing your flow activities? Is your pleasure seeking in balance with your flow?

Big Peace Day 32: What Do I Want?

'As soon as you trust yourself you will know how to live.' – Goethe

I have a theory that often we are out of flow in our lives because we've got out of the habit. We grew up living our lives by someone else's rules, and put our lives on hold while we deal with a long list of shoulds so that we never have time to indulge our own 'flow'.

Do you REALLY know what gives you a sense of fulfilment and gratification in your life? Today, look at the list below and tick the statements that speak to you:

- ❀ It takes you hours to make a decision (because deep down you haven't got a clue about what you really want/what's really important to you).
- ❀ You constantly end up doing things you don't want to do – and you resent it.
- ❀ You always search for an 'expert' to help you – you never trust your own instincts.
- ❀ You appear to 'have it all' but still feel something is missing.
- ❀ You envy enthusiastic and passionate people – what are they getting so excited about?

✿ You feel directionless.

✿ You dread going to work every day but you do it because it pays the bills.

✿ You hate going clothes shopping because you don't know what suits you.

✿ You find yourself bitching and gossiping about other people because it makes you feel better about your own life.

✿ You're surrounded by people who bitch and gossip about other people. (You're often scared that if you leave the room, then they'll be bitching and gossiping about you.)

If you ticked two or more of the above, it suggests that you're out of touch with the real stuff that will give your life meaning, satisfaction and purpose.

Try this exercise. If you were on your death bed – and had lived the 'ultimate life' – describe that life. Are you married? Who are your friends? What kind of career have you had? What kind of adventures have you had? Write for ten minutes without taking your pen off the paper.

What do you really want to create in this life? It can be specific or it can be more general, but make it heartfelt. Leave what you've written in a drawer and then read it back a few days from now. What is your heart craving to create? A life of significance? To contribute? To simply be loved?

Big Peace Day 33: Finding Your Golden Glow

'There is a vitality, a life-force that is translated through you into action. And because there is only one of you in all time, this expression is unique and if you block it, it will never exist through any other medium and will be lost.' – Martha Graham

Today we are going to identify what gives you a feeling of gratification in your life – a feeling of 'life is good'. I call it the golden glow.

Look back over the past week (or year, if a week doesn't give you enough to work with) and remember ten golden moments – moments that you've loved, moments that have given you a warm, fuzzy glow.

1. Identify the fuzzy moment and what you were doing.
2. Write down what it was you valued in that moment.

As an example, here are my top five golden moments:

Golden moment 1: Waking up and not having to do anything I don't want to do that day. What do I value? Space and freedom.

Golden moment 2: Coaching a client and connecting deeply with that person. I also love talking to my friends. What do I value? Connecting on a deep level with people.

Golden moment 3: Watching inspiring films, listening to inspiring tapes and reading inspiring books. What do I value? Inspiration.

Golden moment 4: Learning how to scuba-dive. What do I value? Learning to master something new.

Golden moment 5: I love brainstorming and coming up with ideas for articles, books and magazines. What do I value? Creating new ideas.

❀ My values are:
❀ Space and freedom.
❀ Connecting with people.
❀ Feeling inspired.
❀ Learning to master new things.
❀ Creating new ideas.

Now list your own values.

NEEDS vs VALUES
When first introduced to the concept of 'golden glow' living, many of my clients get confused between unmet needs and values.

What is the difference between a need and a

value? Our values are what we are naturally attracted to doing if we are left to our own devices. We don't need to be motivated to, say, 'get inspired' or 'learn new things' – we just want to. We CHOOSE to build a life around our values.

On the other hand, our needs are like urgent emotional cravings – we feel we have no choice but to get them met. We are DRIVEN to meet our unmet emotional needs, while our values are based on what we really, really *want* to do.

Values are the currency with which your Inner Coach rewards you for listening.

Unmet needs are the fuel of your Inner Pessimist's fear and desperation.

TEN WAYS TO RECOGNIZE A VALUE

1. You look forward to indulging yourself in activities that are orientated around your values – you don't need to hire anyone to motivate you to do them.
2. You'll probably have engaged in value-driven activities as a child. If creativity is one of your values, you will have written short stories in your spare time. If entertaining is one of your values, you will have tap danced for your aunties.
3. A value-driven activity is something you are naturally interested in – it's the specialist

magazine you'll always buy and look forward to reading.

4. It could be a theme that runs through your life. If 'freedom' is one of your values, you might have a freelance career and travel a lot.

5. When you're doing something that reflects your values, you feel fulfilled and relaxed, not driven and anxious.

6. You'll be having a 'Golden Glow' moment when you do it.

7. A value is something you want to express sooner rather than later.

8. You're naturally good at expressing it.

9. You're not trying to prove anything to anyone.

10. You feel happy when it is fulfilled.

Today, ask yourself:
What are my golden moments?
What are my values?
What would my life look like if I expressed these values every day?

Big Peace Day 34: Shackles On or Shackles Off?

*'You will never realize your best destiny through
the avoidance of fear. Rather, you will realize it
through the exercise of courage, which means taking
whatever action is most liberating to the soul, even
when you are afraid.'* – **Martha Beck,** *Steering by Starlight*

I am a massive fan of Martha Beck, the life coach
who is a regular on *Oprah* and who is wise but also
funny. I have adapted this exercise from her Shackles
on/Shackles off exercise from her book, *Steering by
Starlight*. Today, when you find yourself being pulled
off course by trying to be people-pleasing and doing
all the things that you think you should versus what
you really want, try this exercise.

STEP 1
Think about a place, person or thing that makes
your heart sink, that gives you a 'shackles on'
feeling. When you let this person, place or thing fill
your conscious mind, body and mood, how do you
react and feel?
STEP 2
Now think about a person, place or thing that has
proven to be genuinely good for you – something or

someone that leaves you feeling happy, capable and 'shackles off'. When you let this person, place or thing fill your conscious mind, your body and mood, how do you react and feel?

STEP 3

Today, make an action plan to see/do and be around more of the 'shackles off' situations and fewer of the 'shackles on' situations.

Big Peace Day 35: Leap from External to Internal Judgement

'Our character is what we do when we think no one is looking.' – Anonymous

External judgement systems tend to measure our value by what we have, do or look like. As children we learn to measure our worth in the world by what our caregivers tell us about ourselves. If we were held to their breasts, told that we were geniuses, that we were the best, and were treated as such, we would have gone out into the world fairly confident. If we were shouted at and told we were idiots or stupid, lazy or incompetent, then perhaps we might have believed it was true.

Then we went to school and we were judged on our exam results, how well we did in the football or netball team, or perhaps by what trainers (or day-glo socks) we wore in the playground.

Then we grew up and became adults and perhaps learned to measure our value by how much we earn, what job we do, the car we drive, the clothes we wear.

More recently, currency such as fame, how thin, beautiful and young-looking we are has started to become valued highly in society. If you're young, thin, rich and famous, everyone wants to be in your gang.

What if you're not? What if you're a size 22, you can't sing or dance, you're unemployed and you've got your first wrinkle? Does this mean you're not valuable? How many of us believe that to be valuable, to be seen as a success in the world, we have to conform to a certain stereotype? Or earn a certain amount of money? Or look a certain way?

What if you don't conform to what is valued in society? Are you then worthless? Should you feel bad about yourself? Today, we're going to ponder: **how exactly do we measure our value in the world?**

How do you measure your value when external judgement systems are telling you that to be valuable as an employee, employer, mother, father, married person, single person, human being you must have certain qualities or be A, B and C, or have this kind of hair or this kind of car or that kind of mother – and you don't conform?

Today, I want you to consider an alternative. What would you measure yourself against if you didn't have an external measuring tape? How would you know you were doing OK? Or, to put it another way: If you weren't looking to others to see how you were doing, how would you know how you were doing?

> What is valuable to you is what you place value upon.

What do you class as valuable in a human being? Imagine walking into a party and everyone being dressed in fairly anonymous clothes. Now imagine you can't ask what anyone does for a living. How would you decide whether you liked them or not? Strip all the externals away. What do you value in other people? Their humour, their kindness, their intelligence, their gentleness, their creativity? What don't you like? When I had a birthday party recently, I realized that most of my friends are very creative. I obviously value that highly – in others, and in myself.

If you had to score yourself on the qualities you value, how would you fare? What's your opinion of yourself? Do you like yourself? Why? Why not? What bits do you like about yourself? What bits don't you like? What would it be like if we did a 180-degree mind shift and, rather than having to prove how good you are to other people, it were up to you to decide how valuable you are based on your own measuring system? I think creativity is important, but that might be totally irrelevant as a measuring system for you.

As we've discussed, many of our beliefs about ourselves are formed as we grow up. We pick them up from our parents, our teachers, our peers. So what beliefs did you pick up? Were you the clever one of the school, the kind one of the family, the happy one of the gang, the grumpy one of the siblings, the interesting one of the class? Beliefs become true for us when we find evidence to support those beliefs. For instance, if you have a belief that you are clever, you will probably have a barrage of evidence to show that this is true – top marks from classes you've taken, teachers who praised you, friends who copied your homework, perhaps.

So if we're lucky, we've gathered lots of evidence which tells us we are wonderful, we are loved for exactly who we are, not for what we do. If we're lucky, we were brought up to believe that we were worthwhile human beings.

But what if we weren't? Does that mean we're not? Does that mean we're doomed to spend a life with a low opinion and value of ourselves? Does it mean that we have to conform to the external judgement systems to earn our place in the world? Earn more, eat less and have beautiful hair – to prove that we're 'worth it'?

Don't get me wrong; low self-esteem can be a very strong driver in accruing the external trappings of success. I coach many successful high-fliers who have the fundamental belief of 'I'm not good enough,' and to prove that they are, they achieve, achieve and achieve. I AM VALUABLE, their clothes, car, house, job title scream to the world.

The only downside with this approach is that, take away the external trappings of success, and you can feel 'like a nobody'. This kind of value can be taken away from you, and you can be in a constant state of fear wondering when that time will come – when someone will catch you out and see you for the fake you really are. Will you ever HAVE enough to feel that you ARE enough?

What has to happen for you to decide that you are enough and highly valuable just as you are?

Let's work with that question today.

Let's think about how you treat yourself. First, though, think about how you treat the people that you love. Do you expect your children or best friend or partner to work 16 hours a day? Do you feed them junk food day in and day out and encourage them to drink coffee to get them going when they're tired? How do you speak to the people you love? Do you treasure them, praise them, tell them why they're so lovely? Or are you constantly criticizing them and telling them why they are so terrible and how they deserve everything they get because they're just so rubbish at life? Do you love your favourite people for who they are rather than what they do for you?

Today, answer the follow questions:

- ❧ How do you treat someone you value? And how do you treat yourself? What's the gap?
- ❧ Complete the sentence: *If I valued myself I would ...*
- ❧ Answer the question: Who would you need to be to really value yourself? (e.g. Truthful? Kind? Loving? A person of integrity?)
- ❧ What five new standards for life would you follow if you were to live the values that you feel are important? (e.g. Always say the kindest thing? Always choose the most loving response, even when you disagree? Always be brave? Always tell the truth?)

Week 6

Are You Happy Now?

*'Often people attempt to live their lives backwards:
they try to have more things or more money, in order
to do more of what they want so that they will be
happier. The way it actually works is the reverse. You
must first be who you really are, then, do what you
need to do, in order to have what you want.'*

– Margaret Young

When I first started on my very determined search for
inner peace, I decided I wasn't going to set any goals
for a year – and my intention was to 'just be'! All I
felt was panic.

What? No bright future to create, no new goals to
reach? Without something to aim for, I felt incredibly
flat. I was shocked to discover how much my life had
been focused on the future.

I was like one of those annoying people at a party,
trying to focus on what's right in front of them but
constantly looking past it to see if there was a more
interesting future coming into the room.

119

The 'happiness scientists' say it's my brain that is to blame. It's back to that reptilian brain wiring, which uses negative emotions such as fear to prompt us to take action to ensure survival, which in the twenty-first century translates as a driving search for possessions and accomplishments to make us bigger, better and faster. The scientists call it the 'hedonic treadmill'.

I was on the self-improvement hedonic treadmill. It wasn't so much a bigger or better car that I was running after. It was more about the self-improvement goals or what I call the 'I'll be happy when' goals. You know the ones – I'll be happy when I'm thinner/have whiter teeth/have written a best-seller/have done more/when I *am* more. I soon realized that my 'search' for inner peace was just more of the same: 'I'll be happy when I'm more peaceful/calm/when I've 'found' my zen place, where I'd smile serenely and wave regally from some exalted 'there'.

Depressingly, after ten years of my own self-improvement project, I realized I was still holding up great big hoops for me to jump through, and still measuring my self-worth on whether or not I achieved a, b and c. My aim had been increasingly focused on the destination, a magical place called 'there' where I would be transformed. But like the end of the rainbow, whenever I ran towards it, it was always beyond the next hill.

I felt frustrated and confused, so I hit the gym and started pounding the real treadmill, hoping for inspiration. Afterwards, red-faced with the effort, I slumped into a chair and Pam, a woman in her 60s who was glowing after a yoga session, started to chat to me. 'Great to stretch my aching bones,' she said. I murmured sympathetically about getting older. 'Oh no, this isn't old age, I've just come back from sailing round the world.'

We chatted some more and I discovered she'd done everything from fostering over 70 children to high-fashion modelling. Oh, and she was just finishing writing her book. 'You've had an amazing life,' I sighed. She looked at me beadily. 'I'm *having* an amazing life,' she said. And off she went for a swim.

The penny finally dropped. The amazing life was here and I was missing it, running after the next rainbow. I decided I didn't want to run any more – especially on this treadmill of my own making.

I needed help, so I turned to Marianne Williamson. She had just written her new book *The Age of Miracles*, all about embracing what she calls the 'new midlife'.

'Once you're past a certain age, you can hardly believe you wasted even one minute of your youth not enjoying it,' she laughs. 'And the last thing you want to do now is steal any more life from yourself by failing to be deeply in it,' she advises. 'This moment is all you have.'

She told me to stop searching outside myself for peace, either in the past or the future. 'You are who you are, not who you might be one day. Your life is what it is, not what it might be someday. And by focusing on who you are and what your life is right now, you come to the ironic and almost amusing realization that, yes, the fun is in the journey itself.'

And why on earth would I want to spend that journey on an interminably boring treadmill, red-faced and panting trying to get 'there', when all the interesting stuff is going all around me?

What I've realized is that there is no 'there'. The place of transformation is right here. In the present. No more hoops, no more rainbows, no more running, no more treadmills.

Which leaves us with the challenge of living in the now.

Which is what Week 6 is all about.

Big Peace Day 36: What Do You Really Want?

'I've a feeling we're not in Kansas any more.'
– Dorothy in *The Wizard of Oz*

Today I invite you to take a trip to La-La Land. There are only two rules: First, you must never wonder how you are going to do it for real (that's not allowed), and second, anything goes – you can move to a different country or even fly to the moon if you wish! Your vision of La-La Land must make you laugh out loud, and feel exhilarated and slightly bashful. Now complete the following exercise.

A journalist from one of the biggest and best-selling magazines in the land is coming to interview you. You are living your La-La Land life. Write your answers down.

- ✿ Why does such a prestigious magazine want to interview you? What have you achieved?
- ✿ The interviewer has written a description of your lifestyle. Read the description. How does the journalist describe you? What are you wearing? How old do you look?
- ✿ The journalist wants to know about your love life and family life. How do you describe these parts of your life?

❀ The journalist wants to write a paragraph about your average day. Paint a picture of a typical day.

❀ Describe the big highlight of this year for you. How did it make you feel?

❀ On your journey to achieving all you have in La-La Land, you've had some 'crunch' moments, when you've made decisions that got you to this place. Describe some of your turning-point moments.

❀ If you to were to give one piece of advice to your readers, what would it be?

❀ The journalist asks you about your vision for the future. What is it?

❀ The journalist asks what kind of legacy you would like to leave behind? What is it?

In my La-La Land, I've written an Oscar-winning screenplay, have won the Man Booker Prize and have created an *Oprah*-style web portal in the UK that inspires people every day. What kind of life do you live in your La-La Land?

The next question I want to ask you is: If you were living it large in La-La Land, with all the things, people and maybe that beautiful yacht that you think would make you happy, how are you hoping it might make you feel? Free? Loved? Secure? Respected?

The Big Leap in thinking is realizing that the yacht won't make you feel free, it will just take you from A to B and will probably be great fun to sail. However, you can have freedom in your life right now by changing the way you think.

Freedom, peace, love – they are internal states.

I know it's a leap. I know I'd be so happy if I won that Oscar! But for how long? I thought I'd be happy when I became a journalist, when I became health editor of a national magazine, when I became a successful coach, when I became a mother, when I moved to the country – and I was and am. But then I'm scanning the horizon for more. Back on that hedonic treadmill, running faster and faster.

Many of us may think winning prizes or earning more money will make us happy. But no, this is simply not true. Nobel Prize-winning researcher Dr Daniel Kahneman PhD found that it's a complete myth that wealth brings happiness.

On research into people's reported happiness and life satisfaction, he found that people are likely to overrate the joy-bringing effect of whatever they're thinking about at the time, whether it's money or the number of dates they had last week.

What he discovered was that increases in income actually have a relatively brief effect on life satisfaction; that when countries experience a sudden increase in income, there is not a corresponding increase in citizens' sense of wellbeing. Life satisfaction does tend to increase as a nation's per-capita income rises, but there is little increase in life satisfaction once per-capita income goes above $12,000 a year.

Finally, studies show that the wealthier people are, the more intense negative emotions they experience. These studies do not link wealth with greater experienced happiness. Be careful what you wish for!

Things, money, a fancy lifestyle will not make us feel peaceful or happy in the long run. But we long for them because we think they will make us FEEL differently.

So today, choose to feel differently anyway. Try this visualization.

Think of someone or a place or a time when you felt completely at peace. Where are you? What are you doing? What can you see? What can you hear? What can you smell? You're feeling peaceful – where are you feeling it in your body? Let that feeling expand up, down and sideways, let it flow out the top of your head, through your feet. How does it feel?

Who needs a yacht? (Actually I know someone whose yacht really does make him happy, but more about him tomorrow.)

Big Peace Day 37: Setting Goals in the Present

'Every morning, when we wake up, we have 24 brand-new hours to live.' – Thich Nhat Hanh

Yesterday we were considering the thought that what we imagine will make us happy might do so, but only briefly until we see the next thing we want, and the next thing and the next. So we end up running on that hedonic treadmill, going nowhere, never fully gratified, never at peace.

I'm not saying we can't set goals. Just not 'I'll be happy when' goals. My La-La Land vision is based on my values – creativity, inspiration, connecting with others. Yes, yes, it would be lovely to win an Oscar, but in the meantime I can still enjoy living my values by setting goals that make me happy every day, ones that I will enjoy engaging with on a daily basis.

My brother's hobby is sailing. He loves it, so for him buying a yacht wasn't some luxury item that was about showing how big and clever he was, but a way that he could engage in his hobby every weekend and summer – if you can call it summer on the north-east coast of England!

This book is another example. Instead of setting out to find a publisher and write a new book, I simply started writing my Big Peace blog and enjoying writing every day. It got to a point where I really wanted to write the book, so I pitched it to a publisher. But it was something I wanted to do rather than thought I *needed* to do to get me something.

The distinction is enjoying the journey versus it being all about the destination. This distinction gives you permission to start small, and allows you to enjoy thoroughly, for example, learning how to run a five-kilometre race and working up to your local ten-kilometre fun run, congratulating yourself on every step rather than waiting until you've run the London Marathon before you can feel like you've achieved
something.

Today, answer the following:

What goals can you set that are about enjoying the present?

How can you express your values right here, right now? If your La-La Land was about climbing Everest, ask – what does that give you? Adventure? Freedom? What goal can you set which has you being adventurous and free on a daily basis?

Big Peace Day 38: No, Really, Do it Now

'Do what you can, with what you have, where you are.' – **Theodore Roosevelt**

Today, we're going to be focusing even more on the present.

Ask yourself what will make the biggest improvement to your life right now. Ask yourself what you desperately need that you're not getting. Hot water for your evening bath because your boiler's broken? Extra childcare so you can spend some time with your partner? A day in bed sleeping? What would be your top five wishes?

Now take action, in the next 60 minutes, that will make these five wishes a reality. Log on and book appointments with your local day-care nurseries, find a plumber or babysitter, talk to your boss and book time off work.

All change takes place in the present, so make a decision and commit to getting what you need right now.

Big Peace Day 39: Stroke Your Cat

'Think big thoughts, but relish small pleasures.'
– H Jackson Brown, Jr

Today we're going to flood your body with endorphins – these are the natural feel-good hormones that relax you, anaesthetize pain and are responsible for a feeling of wellbeing. Unlike dopamine, these hormones make you feel content and satisfied.

William Bloom, one of Britain's top holistic teachers and author of *The Endorphin Effect*, studied and taught meditation for years but was thrown when people in his meditation classes said they felt just as good stroking their cat (or riding their motorbike/ going for a lovely walk) as they did meditating.

This led Bloom to research what is now known as the 'endorphin effect' – how relaxed, loved up and peaceful you feel when your body is flooded with endorphins.

Bloom's research has shown that are five ways you can trigger these endorphins – without meditating – to feel good NOW, no matter what is going on in your life:

1. Think about someone you like or do something you like. (Make a list of things you

genuinely enjoy and do more of them – this will naturally trigger a flood of endorphins.)

2. Make napping your greatest skill. Or at least allow your body to slump and your body language to sink into napping body language. A three- or four-minute slump will release that flood of feel-good hormones.

3. Twenty minutes of movement – it doesn't have to be aerobic; any sustained movement for 20 minutes or more will release endorphins.

4. Connect with nature – be it staring at a blade of grass or going for a walk in the woods. This is proven to release endorphins in the body.

5. Monitor how your body feels and give it a break – treat it as you would a hurt animal or child – gently relax and think loving, kind thoughts about your poor old body. Apparently, every time we do this, endorphins flood to the rescue.

Big Peace Day 40: Focus on the Details

'True life is lived when tiny changes occur.' – **Leo Tolstoy**

Today we are going to sweat the small stuff. Or focus on the details, at least.

Today we are not going to focus on the big picture; instead, we're going to start cleaning up the details in our life. Details generally occur in the present and you can do something about them without being paralysed with fear or analysing the fluff in your navel.

Today spend 60 minutes creating a system to make your life run more smoothly. From putting all your bills on to direct debit to having a special place in your hallway/desk/handbag where your mobile phone and keys always live. An hour a day working 'on' your life rather than 'in' your life can create spectacular results.

Big Peace Day 41: What Was the Best Bit of Your Day and Why?

'The Force is what gives a Jedi his power. It's an energy field created by all living things. It surrounds us and penetrates us. It binds the galaxy together.'
– **Obi Wan Kenobi,** *Star Wars*

This technique I learned from my lovely Danish friend Lissen Marschall (www.LissenM.com). Lissen runs her own jewellery business and supports her author husband Michael Booth as he travels around the world writing his travel and food books while, at the same time, looking after her two boys Asger and Emil.

They live a full-on life that could be fairly stressful, but every dinner time, wherever they are in the world, the family sits together and answers the question 'What was the best bit of your day and why?' It is a brilliant way to focus all their minds on what was good about the day, and to get the kids and adults alike explaining why something was good and why it was important to them.

I brought that technique home from Denmark and my son Charlie and I use it every day. Not only is it delightful to hear that wrestling on the bed with his light sabre was the best bit of Charlie's day (ah, the joy of simple pleasures), it has created a positive focus to our meal times and time together.

You don't have to do it with kids – or just at meal times.

It's a great end-of-the-day/-week practice to incorporate into your life.

Studies have shown that taking time each day to write down the things that went well and why works brilliantly to make us feel less depressed and happier.

What we focus on expands.

Big Peace Day 42: Be Grateful

'The more you praise and celebrate your life, the more there is to celebrate.' – Oprah Winfrey

Today I want to introduce you to a scientifically proven method to make you feel happier, more peaceful and healthier. All you have to do is focus and write down what you're grateful for.

At the University of California at Riverside, psychologist Sonja Lyubomirsky showed how a gratitude journal – a diary in which subjects write down things for which they are thankful – made participants happier after only six weeks. She has found that taking the time, once a week, conscientiously to count one's blessings can significantly increase a person's overall satisfaction with life.

Gratitude exercises can do more than lift one's mood. At the University of California at Davis, psychologist Robert Emmons found they improve physical health, raise energy levels and, for patients with neuromuscular disease, relieve pain and fatigue. 'The ones who benefited most tended to elaborate more and have a wider span of things they're grateful for,' he notes.

In his book, *Thanks! How Practicing Gratitude Can Make You Happier*, Dr Emmons describes gratitude as a two-part process. Part one is acknowledging the goodness in our lives; part two is recognizing that the source of this goodness exists 'at least partially' outside us. He says it is an awareness that we are on the receiving end of goodness and that there are people out there who are generous, loving and kind. Emmons noted that people who take the time to record their reasons for giving thanks report feeling more loving, forgiving, joyful and enthusiastic. Their families reported that they seem happier and are more pleasant to be around.

The research also discovered that conscious practice of gratitude encourages reciprocal kindness among people, since one act of gratitude encourages another.

Why does it work? Some forms of depression are caused by a habit of negative thinking. Depression is inner-focused, self-focused, whereas gratitude is an outward projection. By focusing on gratitude, we become aware of the positive aspects of our lives, and this can affect our very outlook on life – and start building new positive neural pathways in the brain.

Today, create your own gratitude journal. Start out with a plain, blank notebook. Throughout your day, consciously look for things for which you are grateful and make mental notes. The key is to start out by acknowledging the small things such as 'The sky looked so beautiful this morning on my way to work' or 'I love the way the air smells this time of year.' When you begin by recognizing the small, ordinarily overlooked blessings in your life, the more substantial gifts such as, 'I am lucky to have someone who loves me for who I am' or 'I have a great family' will be easier to recognize and record. Now, before you go to bed each night, make it a habit to write down at least five things in your notebook from your day that you are grateful for. Try to be consistent with the time and place you do your journalling each night so you develop a habit.

Take this exercise further by looking for the positive angle in all things throughout your day. View challenges and obstacles as opportunities; look for the silver lining.

Week 7

How Slow Can You Go?

'What do you like doing best in the world, Pooh?'

'Well,' said Pooh, 'what I like best –' and then he had to stop and think. Because although Eating Honey was a very good thing to do, there was a moment just before you began to eat it which was better than when you were, but he didn't know what it was called. And then he thought that being with Christopher Robin was a very good thing to do, and having Piglet near was a very friendly thing to have; and so, when he had thought it all out, he said, 'What I like best in the whole world is Me and Piglet going to see You, and You saying "What about a little something?" and Me saying, "Well, I shouldn't mind a little something, should you, Piglet?" and it being a hummy sort of day outside, and birds singing.'

'I like that too,' said Christopher Robin, 'but what I like doing best is Nothing.'

'How do you do Nothing?' asked Pooh, after he had wondered for a long time.

'Well, it's when people call out at you just as you're going off to do it, "What are you going to do, Christopher Robin?" And you say "Oh, nothing," and then you go and do it.'

'Oh, I see,' said Pooh.

'This is a nothing sort of thing that we're doing now.'

'Oh, I see,' said Pooh again.

'It means just going along, listening to all the things you can't hear, and not bothering.'

'Oh,' said Pooh.

– A A Milne, *The House at Pooh Corner*

Our obsession with speed, with cramming more in, living life in the fast lane, means that we race through life instead of actually living it. Everything suffers – our health, diet and relationships. We mess up at work. We can't relax, enjoy the moment; we even find sleeping difficult.

So imagine how you would feel if someone told you that you'd done enough and could simply relax now. That you could step off the treadmill, take a load off, and 'just be'? I nearly choked on my extra-strong espresso when I heard this little gem. I haven't got time to just 'be', sweetie, I said. I had deadlines to meet, people to chivvy and a gigantic list of things to do, do, do.

My life was about lists and magazine articles torn out because they contained some awfully good ideas, and things filed for future reference and projects half-finished and 'things in the pipeline'. I was so busy I was a blur. 'Why are you so busy?' asked the insistent voice. 'Because I have so much do, do, do,' I replied, ordering another espresso to go.

My life was filled to the brim – with no space to breathe, to think. Keep running and I'll get to the finishing line, I thought. If only I knew where it was. I just need to know more, do more, be more, I thought. Then I can slow down.

But do we ever really get there? Have we ever done enough? Do we ever get to the place when we think, 'Ah, yes, I've finally done enough, I can relax now.' What would happen if you were enough just exactly the way you are?

Talk like this would just have me sprinting faster. My fear? If I slowed, if I threw away my things-to-do list, I would be nothing. I would have nothing to hide behind. All the busy-ness, the stress, stress, stress gave me something to hide behind. They gave me an identity. And in a strange way, made me feel important. Being busy made me feel like I had a life, that I was in demand, that there was some meaning to my life. Strip it all away and then what? Who would I be? The doing defined my 'being', as it were. And without the doing, I was afraid my 'being' wouldn't exist. So when I began to slow down, I didn't find it very easy. I was facing my worst fears. So I'm not saying this week is going to be easy for you, but perhaps you're not as barmy as me.

This week, we're on a go-slow week. Many of us actually don't do this unless we are ill or on holiday. At first, I found it almost impossible. To be still, to sit and just 'be'. My thoughts were like a spider in the bath. I felt I only had one speed – FAST. But I'm slowly discovering a new pace – it's very idle and it's very lovely, and this week I hope you'll join me in downing tools and riding in the slow lane for a few days. How slow can you go?

Big Peace Day 43: Join the Slow Movement

'What is this life if, full of care,
We have no time to stand and stare?' – **W H Davies**

Have you heard of the Slow Movement – it's gathering force (but not speed)? Founded over 20 years ago by Carlo Petrini, the Slow Movement started as a foodie fightback against the opening of a McDonald's restaurant on Rome's Spanish Steps – but has now mushroomed over the whole gamut of life – be it eating, work, food – even sex. (Yes, there's even an official Slow Sex movement!)

The Slow Movement is about slowing down and taking time to enjoy the things that give us pleasure. It's about reconnecting with food, people and places. It's not about consistently going at a snail's pace, but just encouraging you to take the scenic route every now and again. Carl Honoré says in his book, *In Praise of Slow*, 'The secret is balance. Instead of doing everything faster, do everything at the right speed. Sometimes fast. Sometimes slow. Sometimes somewhere in between.'

Let me be your slow coach today.

Try the following questions:

❈ If 100 miles an hour is top speed in your engine, what speed do you usually travel? What would have to change in your life (more childcare, more support from the boss, better systems in place – direct debits/weekly babysitter, etc.) for you to change gear and slow down every now and again?

❈ What are you trying to prove by driving so fast in life?

❈ What would you have to believe about yourself to slow down?

❈ When during your day/week/year would be a good time to change gear, slow down and try a different pace/have a pit stop?

Big Peace Day 44: How Can You Increase the Currency of Slow in Your Life?

'For lack of attention a thousand forms of loveliness elude us every day.' – Evelyn Underhill

Often we find it hard to slow down because we believe 'Faster is better.' Sometimes fast is best – I love my speedy broadband connection; I love prompt service when I eat out; I love driving fast on a motorbike.

But some things are definitely better slow – be it a morning in bed with your loved one or a day idling in the park with the kids and the dog.

Not that I'm saying that I don't enjoy fast food and even fast sex – sometimes. It is about being able to change gear, to slow down, to stall, to come to a complete standstill without my engine completely jamming.

Today, ask yourself: where is slow best?

Where does travelling slowly in your life become as necessary and powerful as 'fast' seems to be? For example, are your 'slow' times when you become your most creative, when you have your best sex, when you sleep the most blissfully?

How can you increase the currency of slow in your life?

Day 45: What Does Your Diary Say about You?

'For a long time it seemed to me that life was about to begin – real life. But there was always some obstacle in the way, something to be gotten through first, some unfinished business, time still to be served, a debt to be paid. At last it dawned on me that these obstacles were my life. This perspective has helped me to see there is no way to happiness. Happiness is the way. So treasure every moment you have and remember that time waits for no one.' – Souza

Today I want you to look at your diary and ask yourself: If a stranger were to look at your diary/schedule in a 'through the keyhole' type of experiment, what would it say about you?

Are you a VERY IMPORTANT PERSON with a VERY IMPORTANT CAREER, are you a selfless mum/dad who needs to give your all to your kids? Are you both?

Try and look at your schedule/diary objectively. What message does your schedule give to the outside world?

Just spend one minute completing this sentence on a piece of paper: My diary/schedule shows to the world that I am ... (a screw-up? very successful? very popular? very loved? very disorganized? in control? master of your own destiny?)

Be honest.

What role does the busy-ness (or non-busy-ness) serve in your life?

How does this serve you?

What does this cost you?

If you didn't have to prove anything to anyone any more – what would you do tomorrow?

Big Peace Day 46: Slow Down Slowing Down

'The time to relax is when you don't have time for it.'
– Sidney J Harris

If you're a rush-aholic and want to slow down, your first impulse may be to try too hard and expect instant results. Making a change takes time and isn't always easy. The fear of slowing down can really be a fear of confronting yourself, as I discovered, so decelerate in increments.

Today, simply take a slow hour. What would it be like to spend an hour completely free from any pressing matter? Make sure you keep this date with yourself. How will you use your slow hour? Will you be tempted to fill it up with striking things off your to-do list, or will you be able to slow down? Do you have to try it and find out? Will you feel guilty about taking care of yourself?

Big Peace Day 47: Become a Sleep Slut

'As a well-spent day brings happy sleep, so a life well spent brings happy death.' – Leonardo da Vinci

Today, book time out – and instead of doing all the jobs that need doing, take to your bed, lie there and close your eyes. Some of us will find this task really easy (I'm a highly skilled sleep slut – napping is my most treasured skill), but others will find this a 'waste of time'. I need you all to work through your resistance and experiment with the joy of napping.

Remember that you'll be in good company: John F Kennedy, Winston Churchill, Thomas Edison, Napoleon Bonaparte and Leonardo da Vinci were all highly skilled nappers.

About half the world takes an afternoon siesta. It's a biological thing, not just a cultural one: body temperature and alertness dip during mid-afternoon, which makes it a perfect time to rest your weary head. But don't sleep for too long.

A study at Flinders University in Australia has shown we're much better off snatching ten minutes of sleep than taking a more leisurely 30 minutes, as ten minutes results in quicker improvements in mood, alertness and mental performance than 30-minute naps.

And simply do not underestimate the value of
sleep. 'Because we live in a 24-hour rat race where
sleep is not valued, one in four of us are chronically
sleep deprived,' says James Maas, author of *Power
Sleep* and the social psychologist who coined the
now-famous phrase 'power nap'. He says: 'With
heavy demands of work, household chores, parenting
and family responsibilities and a desire for a social
life, exercise and recreation, we are cutting back on
sleep to gain time for what seems more important
or interesting. This can be a dangerous and costly
mistake.'

He may be right. Experts agree that sleep
deprivation will make you irritable, depressed,
stressed and anxious, reduce your immunity to
disease and viral infections, make you feel lethargic
and generally have you piling on the pounds as you
reach for sugary foods to help you stay awake.

Not forgetting, of course, reduced ability to make
decisions, concentrate, remember, handle complex
tasks or think logically and critically, reduced
creativity and just generally poorer coordination. And
that's the good news. The bad news is that total sleep
deprivation will kill you in the end. Sleep, like food,
is a biological must; without it, we'll simply fade
away. A now-famous experiment at the University of
Chicago deprived rats of sleep for a week or more.

The poor, sleepless creatures didn't just stumble around. They died.

So stop resisting, take your shoes off, loll on the bed and snooze.

Big Peace Day 48: Create a Nourish-me Zone

'I have an everyday religion that works for me: love yourself first and everything else falls into line.'
– **Lucille Ball**

I've discovered that you can't do fast nourishing. It has to be done at a slow, kind pace. It can't be hurried.

Today, ask yourself: if you could improve your wellbeing by nourishing your mind, body and soul – how would you do that? From eating cake in the bath to switching your mobile phone off and sitting in a church or a wood or a park, what can you eat that makes you feel completely nourished? Who are the people that nourish you? How can you spend more time with them? What books nourish you? What places nourish you?

Complete these lists:
❀ The people who nourish me are ...
❀ The places that nourish me are ...

❀ The things that nourish me are …
❀ The thoughts that nourish are …
❀ The activities that nourish me are …

Now choose one today and indulge yourself.

Big Peace Day 49: Slow Inspiration

'Most of us are yearning to reconnect with our inner tortoise.' – Carl Honoré, *In Praise of Slow*

Today, try one of these:
❀ Read a newspaper without switching on the TV.
❀ Read *In Praise of Slow* by Carl Honoré – and be inspired how we can live more productive, fulfilling lives by embracing the philosophy of Slow.
❀ Cook a meal from scratch.
❀ Take a walk with a friend.
❀ Eat dinner with friends at the table, not in front of the TV.
❀ Do one thing at a time!
❀ Turn off the television and stare into space instead.
❀ Take up yoga.
❀ Take up gardening.
❀ Try knitting, painting, reading …

Week 8

Are You Willing to Let It Out?

'Everybody hurts. Everybody cries. Sometimes.' – REM

The Big Peace is not about faux positive thinking. I want your smile to reach your eyes. I don't want you to have that rictus grin with that tilt of your head that makes you look like you've joined a cult.

This process is not about being doggedly positive when you feel like you've been run over by a truck. This book demands – yes, demands – that you get real, because as we all know, bad things do happen to good people.

I went to a Marianne Williamson seminar recently. She's pretty cool and one of my personal favourites. We're talking high-end metaphysical spirituality – forgiveness, not judging others, and learning to love each other. I couldn't wait to see her.

But as I waited in the queue to get in, I just wanted to walk away again. I was about as judgemental as it was possible to be. For waiting outside were a few people who made me feel so angry, I found my top lip trembling in an effort to keep from sneering.

Some were chanting noisily in the queue, making strange shapes with their faces. Others sprayed lavender water around themselves and squirted it over me and smiled 'lovingly', tilting their heads. One woman was sitting in a yoga pose in the middle of the floor and people kept almost tripping over her. If I still smoked, I would have lit up a cigarette, blown smoke all over her and tapped ash on her head.

What was going on? I realize that I was being very judgemental but what galled me was that these people seemed fake. The Big Peace to me is not about spraying, chanting and accessorizing your outfit with the right-coloured yoga mat. The Big Peace has a very strong, powerful, authentic presence that makes you turn round and stare when it walks in a room. The Big Peace doesn't need to draw attention to itself, it's magnetic enough already.

The reason I love Marianne Williamson is that she is very real and her words ooze truth and authenticity. Life can be tough sometimes, and Marianne tells it how it is.

The Big Peace is not about covering up your real feelings. If you do, all that will happen is that it will sit like a huge steaming turd in the middle of your living room. No one mentions it but it slowly suffuses your life with its rancid smell. You can't hide away your pain with a happy smiling 'Let's look on the bright side.'

Sometimes there isn't a bright side. Life can throw us some tough calls. We lose people we love, your husband sleeps with someone else, your wife stops loving you, you watch your mother die and see her flesh fade from her bones, you miscarry for the seventh time …

Pain. It's there. Sometimes you just can't avoid it. We've all got our story. We've all got our pain. But what do we do with it? Just smile a brittle smile and look on the bright side of life? Or do we become defined by it? Orphan, widower, infertile, depressed, unemployed. Do we bury it and just 'get over it'? I suggest we do none of the above, but simply go through it. Feel it and get to the other side of it.

We need to give ourselves time to heal, to let time go by, to feel all the feelings that perhaps you were never allowed to feel because you just had to keep it together. You just have to wallow for a while, honour it, feel it.

I used to think my grief would destroy me (I lost my parents to cancer fairly early on in life). 'I can't bear this,' I thought. I'd anaesthetize myself with anything I could – food, alcohol, cigarettes – to numb me out. I felt like there was a black hole of pain inside me that would suck me in; and that would be it, I'd never been seen again. So I made a decision that I would never travel into the black hole. It was just too scary. Instead, I camped right outside it.

We can do drugs, drink, eat junk food, smoke cigarettes, play computer games, watch television, but it's just avoidance. Avoidance of something that feels like it will destroy you. And on some level it does. Pain burns you up, destroys you, leaves you like a shell. But you do survive it. And tomorrow is another day and you are stronger for surviving it, you're stronger for being on your knees. And you're cleaner somehow. Maybe one step nearer to being healed. The heat cauterizes you. You have a scar that's healing but it's no longer a weeping wound that you're trying to hide under a bandage of distraction.

I can see that you're beginning to get alarmed now. And you're right. Who the hell wants to go there? I agree; it's much easier to distract yourself. A bottle of wine or feeling the fear of being alone/the stab of grief/the sadness/the anger? You choose.

I don't know how you feel. But what I do know is that we all have our own tragedies, our own stories, our own shame. But I believe the longer we carry that pain around with us, the heavier it gets, and we have to use all sorts of strategies to help us keep going – whether by spraying lavender water at strangers or drinking a vat of wine, neither of which, ultimately, will ever give us inner peace.

The way out? To feel it. And you're going to feel low and sad and bad. And there's nothing wrong with that. Don't cover it over. The irony is that, to get to a place of peace, we might have to suffer a bit. But I would suggest there is more suffering in the hiding. When we're hiding from our pain, we live our lives in the shadows. By avoiding the very thing we're afraid of, we live half-lives.

Walk through the doorway. Be sad, be angry, feel it. Stop running away from yourself. This is not about being nice or positive. This is about being raw and honest with yourself. No more cover-ups. It's time to be brave. To roar, to burn, to step into the fire. No more hiding, no more 'Have a nice day.' Have a terrible day, go into hibernation and wail, rasp and be real. Let it out.

Get help – you don't have to do it alone. Find someone – a professional or a friend – who can listen to you while you heal so that you don't have to hold it together or hold it in. This week gives you some strategies for letting it out. I'm sending you much love.

Big Peace Day 50: Are You a Freezer, Breezer or a Runner?

'The best way out is always through.'
– Robert Frost

Let it out? If that sounds as appealing as licking your kitchen floor clean, don't worry.

Some of us don't like to talk about our feelings but would rather run from them or bury them deep. Today, we're going to establish if you are one of these people.

Study after study shows that it's not what happens to us but how we handle it that keeps us emotionally healthy and sane in times of stress.

Many of us, however, are unaware of how we are feeling most of the time – because we are not trained to recognize and label our emotions. Do you know how you are feeling for the majority of the time? Like right now, for instance. Ask yourself, how are you? No really, how are you feeling? Are you feeling anxious? Low? Exhausted? Excited? Content? Happy? Can you recognize and label how you're really feeling moment to moment?

For most of us, the answer to that question is 'No.' We can't recognize and label emotions because we spend our life stuffing them down or running away from them – especially our negative ones.

There is a growing body of scientific evidence that isolation and suppression of your feelings can lead to illness, whereas intimacy and social support are healing. However, because we choose to run away or stuff down our feelings rather than express them, situations can often escalate into a crisis until we have no choice – we emotionally 'break down' or become ill.

But many of us are so skilled at running away from our feelings that we're not even aware something's bothering us until it gets really painful and we end up sobbing uncontrollably on the couch. It is, therefore, very useful to be able to spot the symptoms of our emotional style so we can figure out the best way to seek help.

Generally, people fall into three categories in the way they cope with negative emotions. They either run away from them ('runners'), stuff them down ('freezers') or feel them and move on ('breezers').

If you're a runner, you tend to try to avoid your negative feelings by keeping busy. You tend to feel stressed and overwhelmed constantly. You go into a frenzy of activity rather than actually facing how you feel.

If you're a freezer, you cope with stress and negative feelings by anaesthetizing yourself. You are a master at masking how you really feel, not only to others but to yourself. Usually you do this because, if you were to admit to yourself how you feel, you'd have to do something about it – and that means stepping out of your comfort zone. And that makes you feel even more anxious.

If you're a breezer, you tend to 'breeze through life' because, although you struggle with the same life challenges as everyone else, you know how to express your feelings in a healthy way.

Today, ask yourself: How do you usually cope with negative emotions? If you're feeling upset, or angry, or sad, what is your usual way of processing these feelings?

Over the next few days, we're going to explore some healthy ways to deal with powerful emotions.

Big Peace Day 51: Don't Isolate Yourself, Find Your Tribe

'We take our bearings, daily, from others. To be sane is, to a great extent, to be sociable.' – John Updike

Dr James House at the University of Michigan has found that social isolation increases our susceptibility to falling ill. 'It's the ten to 20 per cent of people who say they have nobody with whom they can share their private feelings, or who have close contact with others less than once a week, who are most at risk.'

On the other end of the scale, when the happiness scientists studied the top ten per cent of 'very happy' people, they were the ones who spent the least time alone and the most time socializing.

Today, look into a 'tribe' or community near you that you like the sound of – be it a running club, a local history group or the Church – and make an appointment to go along for a trial visit.

Big Peace Day 52: Cry, You'll Pee Less

'If you haven't cried, your eyes can't be beautiful.'
– Sophia Loren

My no-nonsense Northern granny used to positively encourage me to cry when I was a little girl. 'Go on, cry some more,' she'd yell. 'It's good for you. You'll pee less.'

I'm not sure if it makes you pee less, but according to biochemist William Frey at the St Paul-Ramsey Medical Center in Minneapolis, my granny was right. Crying is good for you. According to Frey, stress hormones are dramatically reduced by crying, as we eliminate them through tears.

Tears are nature's safety valve. Most psychologists and psychiatrists agree that crying is a good way to reduce tension, and that bottling up emotions can lead to health problems. Studies have shown that people who regularly cry suffer fewer gastrointestinal problems, gastric ulcers and attacks of colitis.

If you're a freezer or a runner, you may find this challenging (see Day 50), but sometimes bursting into tears can be the best signal there is that something isn't right. For rude emotional health, we need to stop gulping down our tears and start using them as indicators of what we need to heal and what we need to change.

To get clear about what your tears are telling you, you need to get:

- ❀ Clarity! Describe in one word how you are feeling – sad, overwhelmed, angry.
- ❀ Understanding! What message are your tears giving you? For example, are they telling you that you've had enough of a certain situation or you're still very sad about something that happened in the past?
- ❀ Help! What small baby steps can you take today that will resolve, improve or address the issue? And don't be afraid to ask for help. Whom can you talk to who might know how to handle this? Who can support you while you're healing or dealing with your challenges?

Big Peace Day 53: The Write Way

'My research has shown me that when emotions are expressed – which is to say that the biochemicals that are the substrate of emotion are flowing freely – all systems are united and made whole. When emotions are repressed, denied, not allowed to be whatever they may be, our network pathways get blocked, stopping the flow of the vital feel-good, unifying chemicals that run both our biology and our behavior '. – Dr Candace Pert, *The Molecules of Emotion*

Today I want us to work through an exercise devised by Dr James Pennebaker, psychologist and professor in the Department of Psychology at the University of Texas at Austin. He is author of several books, including *Opening Up* and *Writing to Heal*, and is a pioneer in the study of using expressive writing as a route to healing our emotional ills.

His research has shown that short-term, focused writing can have a beneficial effect on everyone from those dealing with a terminal illness to victims of violent crime to university students facing first-year transitions.

His scientifically measured research shows that 'expressive writing' beneficially affects your immune function, improves blood pressure and even affects your brain waves. And it can have long-reaching positive effects on your life. Pennebaker writes:

'When people are given the opportunity to write about emotional upheavals, they often experience improved health. They go to the doctor less. They have changes in immune function. If they are first-year college students, their grades tend to go up. People will tell us months afterward that it's been a very beneficial experience for them.'

In his early research, Pennebaker was interested in how people who have powerful secrets are more prone to a variety of health problems. If we could find a way for people to share those secrets, would their health problems improve?

It turned out that often they would, and that it wasn't even necessary for people to tell their secrets to anyone else. The act of simply writing about those secrets, even if what was written was destroyed immediately afterwards, had a positive effect on health. Further studies showed that the benefits weren't just for those who had dramatic secrets, but also for those dealing with job rejections or even a difficult commute to work.

Pennebaker explains: 'Emotional upheavals touch every part of our lives. You don't just lose a job, you don't just get divorced. These things affect all aspects of who we are – our financial situation, our relationships with others, our views of ourselves, our issues of life and death. Writing helps us focus and organize the experience.'

Our minds are designed to try to understand things that happen to us. When a traumatic event occurs or we undergo a major life transition, our minds have to work overtime to try to process the experience. Thoughts about the event may keep us awake at night, distract us at work and even make us less connected with other people – robbing us of any peace.

When we translate an experience into language, we essentially make the experience graspable. We may see improvements in what is called 'working memory', essentially our ability to think about more than one thing at a time. We may also find we're better able to sleep. Our social connections may improve, partly because we have a greater ability to focus on someone besides ourselves, says Pennebaker.

Try this exercise for the next four days. It's quite full-on, so follow the instructions below carefully.

❀ For the next four days, write about a trauma or emotional upheaval that profoundly affected your life.

❀ Write for 20 minutes a day.
- If you end up writing for more than 20 minutes, that's great. But you must still write 20 minutes the following day.

❀ Writing topic:
- You can write about the same event on all four days, or about different events each day. Choose to write about something that is extremely personal and important to you.

❀ Write continuously.
- Once you begin writing, write continuously without stopping. Don't worry about spelling or grammar. If you run out of things to say, simply repeat what you've already written.

❀ Write only for yourself.
- You are writing for yourself and no one else. Plan to destroy or hide what you have written when you have finished. Do not turn this exercise into a letter.

❀ The flip-out rule:
- If you feel you cannot write about a particular event because it will 'push you over the edge', then don't write about it. Deal with only those events or situations that you can handle now.

If you have any additional traumatic topics that you can't get to now, you can always deal with them in the future.

WHAT TO EXPECT AFTER WRITING.

Many people can feel saddened or depressed after expressive writing, especially on the first day or two of writing. If this happens to you, it's completely normal.

If possible, plan to have some time to yourself after your expressive writing session to reflect on the issues you have been writing about.

Big Peace 54: Talk about It

'I'm not going to lie down and let trouble walk over me.' – Ellen Glasgow

Talking about your thoughts and feelings can help you deal with times when you feel troubled. If you turn a worry over and over in your mind, the worry can grow. But talking about it can help you figure out what the problem really is, and then you can explore what you can do about it. And being listened to helps you feel that other people care about you and what you have to say.

Friends can be great, but so can a therapist, counsellor or coach. Talking therapies involve speaking with someone who is trained to help you deal with your negative feelings. They can help anyone who is experiencing distress. Talking therapies give you the chance to explore your thoughts and feelings, and the effect these have on your behaviour and mood. Describing what's going on in your head and how that makes you feel can help you notice any patterns; and this can help you work out where your negative feelings and ideas come from, why they are there and what you can do about them. Understanding all this can help you make positive changes by thinking or acting differently. Talking therapies can help people to take greater control of their lives and improve their confidence.

And as we saw on Day 4, there is a growing body of evidence showing that talking therapies not only make you feel better but also structurally change your brain.

Magnetic Resonance Imagery (MRI) studies have shown that talking therapies reduce the activity in the brain that processes painful emotions, and light up those magical prefrontal lobes instead.

Today, either talk to someone about how you feel or book an appointment with a professional listener – be it a counsellor, coach or therapist; or simply do some research into different therapists in your area. Know that there are always people there if you need them.

Big Peace Day 55: Honour Your Loved Ones, and Heartbreak

'However long the night, the dawn will break.'
– African proverb

In the Victorian era, people who had lost a loved one wore black for a year to mourn and honour them. Nowadays we hardly pause for breath after the funeral, divorce or heartbreak.

Today, take some time to think about loved ones you have lost. If you had to create a ceremony of some kind or a physical way to 'honour' this loss, how would you do it? Could you make a photo album, visit a grave, create a bonfire and burn old possessions? How can you celebrate a life or the passing of a relationship?

I'm a great fan of Chinese 'wish' lanterns that you light and then release into the sky. I use them to celebrate at parties, and they're also brilliant when I want to signify that I'm letting go of someone or something in my life. I stand in the garden, light my lantern, and then usually cry as I wave it off into the sky. God knows what the neighbours think. But it works for me.

What would work for you?

Big Peace Day 56: Be Mad, Bad and Miserable

'Pain is like that tree being pruned to make it strong. And beautiful.' – **Nikki Gemmel**

This week we've been working on releasing or transforming painful emotions. But today I'd like you to consider the thought that just because you feel bad doesn't mean you can't be peaceful.

One of the most astonishing discoveries I have made in the past couple of years is that I don't have to be happy to be peaceful. In fact, I realized that one of my major obstacles to peaceful living was my belief that life 'should' be happy/good/pleasant/ enjoyable all the time.

Queen of positive thinking, mantras and affirmations, I had been trained to 'reframe' my thoughts and experiences so that I could feel good whenever I wanted. But you know what? This didn't make me feel happy or peaceful; it made me feel wrong if underneath I really felt irritated, sad, mad or miserable. My thought process went like this: 'I'm irritated/sad/mad/miserable so I'm not doing life right. Quick, what can I do to change how I feel?' And that becomes exhausting.

For me, true peace now means surrendering to both the sorrowful and happy points in my day, knowing it's OK to feel a whole rainbow of emotions – irritation, sadness, anger, happiness, amusement – sometimes all within five minutes. And these feelings pass through like waves – be it intense love while watching my son sleep or irritation with him when he refuses to get out of the car while smearing his chocolate-coated hands on the window.

You may be feeling a little up and down over the next few days, so let 'This too shall pass' be your mantra. Accept that you will feel sad, mad or glad in any given moment and don't start building up great big stories in your head about it. Don't put a magnifying glass over it. Just observe the feeling, identify what it is and then let it float away like a thought bubble. This too shall pass.

Week 9

Are You Willing to Let Go?

'The question is not whether we will die, but how we will live.' – Joan Borysenko

This week we're going to be looking at what we're holding on to and how to let go. And to start this week off in a cheerful mood, we're going to talk about death. I'm not being morbid, but often I think we live in a fog of denial about death. We live our lives and pretend that we have all the time in the world. We think that we're going to live for ever, that life is some permanent state. Or perhaps we just conveniently forget that we're mortal.

I know I do. I lost both my parents to cancer – they both died young, and I swore to myself that I wouldn't forget to live every second, to love the life I had, to live my life to the hilt, to appreciate everybody and everything in it. But then a year or so passes (a second passes) and I find myself grumbling and huffing and puffing and complaining about the small stuff.

I think the Buddhist monks have got it right when, as part of their spiritual practice, they meditate on the idea of a corpse. It is to remind them that nothing is permanent and the route to pain is to try to hold on, to 'grasp' at life – trying to make the insecure, secure, the impermanent, permanent.

Sogyal Rinpoche spells it out in *The Tibetan Book of Living and Dying*: 'Grasping is the source of all our problems. Since impermanence to us spells anguish, we grasp on to things desperately, even though all things change. We are terrified of letting go, terrified, in fact, of living at all, since learning to live is learning to let go.'

Learning to let go. Easy to say. And that's what I want to explore in Week 7 – to prise our fingers from our cherished ideas and concepts, from the things that we think are important, and see if we can stop grasping so tightly. I'm going to be asking pretty big questions this week, but I'm hoping that they will encourage you to lighten your load.

Big Peace Day 57: How Heavy Is Your Load?

'People have a hard time letting go of their suffering. Out of a fear of the unknown, they prefer suffering that is familiar.' – **Thich Nhat Hanh**

Today I want you to do a quick inventory. What baggage are you carrying – emotional (resentment/ grudges/sadness), physical (body weight, clutter, stuff) and mental (old negative beliefs, old thinking that no longer serves you)? Write a list of all the things you'd like to let go of – the physical, emotional and mental.

For each item on your list, ask yourself:

❈ What is the cost of the load?'
❈ Are there any benefits to carrying this baggage? (Does carrying extra weight allow you to hide, does your clutter distract you so you don't have to deal with bigger issues, does believing you're not good enough keep you in your comfort zone?)
❈ And finally, ask yourself: If you could find a way, would you be willing to let go of your load?

Big Peace Day 58: Letting It All Go by Not Knowing How

'Even though you may want to move forward in your life, you may have one foot on the brakes. In order to be free, we must learn how to let go. Release the hurt. Release the fear. Refuse to entertain your old pain. The energy it takes to hang onto the past is holding you back from a new life. What is it you would let go of today?' – **Mary Manin Morrissey**

I have recently discovered a brilliant technique created by consciousness teacher Asara Lovejoy, author of *The One Command*. Her business and technique are actually about manifesting wealth in your life, but I have found the process to be just as brilliantly effective for letting go and surrendering old patterns and beliefs – in a powerful six-step process she calls 'The One Command'. I've also found it one of the most powerful techniques to get to my Big Peace place within minutes.

The One Command is a visualization technique that slows the brain waves to the theta state – that relaxed, daydreaming, hypnotic state we normally experience just before we fall asleep and just after we wake up.

Our brain waves are measured as micro-electrical charges per second. The one we are most familiar with is beta – 13–30 cycles per second, known as our waking, conscious mind. Then there is the alpha state, measured at 7–13 cycles per second. This is known as our meditative or contemplative mind. Theta is 4–7 cycles per second and what Lovejoy calls 'the source mind': 'In theta, you reconnect to your natural, creative intelligence, and disengage from the fearful, limited world view of what is possible. You develop a natural sense of security and trust in the world. The thoughts you have in theta are more powerful than your ordinary thoughts, and they bring about changes in your life quickly and easily.'

Today, try out Lovejoy's six-step process.

Write the names of each of the six steps below on a separate piece of paper:

❃ Ground
❃ Align
❃ Go to Theta
❃ Command
❃ Expand

❄ Receive with Gratitude.

Ask a friend to help you if you can. Place six pieces of paper in a horizontal line on the floor. You are going to stand on each piece of paper and get your friend to read the steps out to you. Stay on each step until you complete your visualization, taking as much time as you need, then move sideways to the next step.

Before you step on Ground, think of something you want in your life – be it inner peace, better health or a relationship. Now close your eyes and keep them closed throughout the process. Have your friend read these directions, slowly at each step, as he or she guides you through the whole process. Stay at each step as long as it takes until you know you are ready to continue.

❄ *Step 1: Ground*

Feel the weight of your body settling down onto the paper beneath your feet. Now imagine roots coming out from the bottom of your feet and send them down, deep, deep into the Earth. Connect with the 'magnetic power' of the Earth, the basis and foundation of all of our support, and imagine that you are wrapping your roots around gold, diamonds and rubies in the centre of the Earth. Feel the power of that energy grounding you and balancing you. Stay here until you feel your body shift into a well-grounded state.

❀ *Step 2: Align*

When you are ready, move sideways to the second step (let your friend guide you if necessary by holding on to your waist), and stand on Align. Imagine all that power of the Earth's energy coming into your body, into your heart. Now take a deep breath and, as you exhale, imagine that the energy is expanding in all directions around you. The breath of your heart is expanding in all directions, above and below, and around in all directions. As you exhale, allow that breath to expand in all directions, aligning you with a feeling of unconditional love.

❀ *Step 3: Go to Theta*

Now move sideways to the third step: Go to Theta. Imagine a golden beam of light, a field of energy flowing into you from the far-distant reaches of the galaxies, flowing down through you and out below you, deep into the Earth. Imagine moving your consciousness up this beam of light, out of the top of your head to above your head, out to the outer edges of the planet, on through the solar system, beyond the galaxy, until you push through the black void of space and into the white light of 'source'. Feel how this feels and amplify that feeling.

🌸 *Step 4: Command*

While thinking of the thing you want to create more of in your life, mentally and silently Command: 'I don't know how I … [fill in the blank, e.g. '… let go of my negative thinking/let go of my addictions/ forgive/create a loving relationship/wellness/ abundance, etc. in my life'] I only know that I do now, and I am fulfilled!'

Take your time to allow this declaration to resonate in your body before you take the next step. I have found this command to be incredibly powerful. Many spiritual teachers talk about surrender and letting go, but I often have struggled with how to actually do that; I have found that my whole conscious mind switches off and relaxes when I say the words 'I don't know how.' This technique allows me to surrender and stop trying to control with my conscious mind, leaving my 'source mind' – my creative, imaginative mind – to come up with the answers. Not that it comes up with answers at this point. I just choose to have faith (which is the 'I only know that I do now' piece) that a solution to any challenge I'm struggling with will present itself. I have discovered that, within hours or days, my creative mind is usually inspired with some solutions and answers. Or I just feel differently about the issue and my focus shifts.

What you focus on expands.

❀ *Step 5: Expand*

While you are still in Theta, imagine what you desire in a bigger way, a great capacity, an expanded version that serves more good that your original idea. For example, if you want to feel more peaceful, imagine what impact that might have on the people around you, the life you might create differently if you lived from this perspective. Think really big! Go wild, watch as new, expanded, bigger ideas arrive. Stay in the process until your vision is as big as it will go. Now move on to Step 6.

❀ *Step 6: Receive with Gratitude*

Imagine that your 'request' has been granted. State in your mind clearly: 'Thank you! It is so!' And experience a sense of gratitude and fulfilment. Remember, your mind does not know the difference between real and imagined.

While in a state of gratitude, imagine moving your consciousness back. Feel the golden beam of light coming gently back into your physical body, and imagine the particles of your vision floating down from source into your body, into the cells of your body and into your DNA itself. Imagine unwinding, unwinding, unwinding all the old limiting ideas and rewinding, rewinding, rewinding a new holographic image of your vision. Imagine a new holographic

image of this life that is your new life replicating
itself in every DNA strand in your body, in every
organ of your body, in every hair follicle of your
body, and in every particle of emotion in your body
and thinking. Feel it, accept it and give thanks.
Take a deep breath and imagine sending your
energy back down into the Earth to 'ground'
yourself. Stretch and flex and take all the time you
need to come, once again, fully awake in the room.
Open your eyes.
Take time to share anything you've discovered
while doing this process with your friend.

Lovejoy recommends that you repeat this process
twice the first time you do it. And then practise every
day until it becomes so natural to you that you can
go through the six steps mentally, instantly, any time
that you wish to change or let go of old behaviours
or thinking patterns. Practise until this becomes an
unconscious internal process.

Big Peace Day 59: Eliminate Three Small Projects

'We must be willing to let go of the life we have planned, so as to accept the life that is waiting for us.' – Joseph Campbell

Today I want you to pick three small projects in your life and eliminate them. For example:

1. Resign from that volunteer position that drains your energy.
2. Give up trying to tile the bathroom yourself and get the experts in.
3. Delegate that project in your in-tray that has sat there for months.

Today, ask yourself: If I were brave, what projects could I let go of?

What phone call do you have to make to make letting go of these projects a reality in the next 48 hours?

Big Peace Day 60: De-Junk Your Life

'Are you polluting the world or cleaning up the mess? You are responsible for your inner space; if humans clear inner pollution, then they will also cease to create outer pollution.' – Eckhart Tolle

Don't estimate the power of de-cluttering and getting rid of junk in your life. Clearing out clutter and living a cleaner, simpler life has become an almost spiritual movement. De-junking is not just about clearing out a few cupboards. On one level, it involves a gradual purging of all the stuff you don't need that is clogging up your house and your life. On another level, it's nothing short of a personal liberation.

People who have de-junked talk about the experience as a turning point which has allowed them to reassess their lives and to feel lighter and more free than they have in years.

Holding on to clutter can be a fear response. You can hide and distract yourself with the muddle that it is your life. Instead of muddling through, try asking yourself what you are scared of.

It can be of the next step, of confronting your boss, of going back to work after having your kids. Today, stop hiding in denial, stop hiding in the clutter and get real. Get out a piece of A4 paper and complete the sentence: 'Right now I'm afraid of …'

Write for ten minutes without taking your pen off the paper. Now you can deal with the real issue, not just the symptoms. Create an action plan of how to confront your fear head on – what do you need to do? Have a conversation with your boss? Talk to a counsellor? Make a scary phonecall?

Now ask: What is your junk currently costing you? This can be a very motivating question. What is your junk costing you – financially, emotionally, energetically and physically? Put a figure on it. When I recently de-junked my household accounts, I discovered my house had not been insured for a whole year – that could have been a very costly mistake!

Now tackle the clutter with this three-question strategy:

- ❀ How are you going to do it?
- ❀ When are you going to do it by?
- ❀ Why are you doing it?

Create a de-junking weekend, or set a time and date and commit to de-junking a corner/drawer/cupboard in one hour with a friend, and then report back on your progress. Friends can help you be more ruthless. Stick the answer to the 'why' question around your house. It is incredibly motivating to know that the real reason you are de-junking is you 'want to make space for wonderful new opportunities to flood into my life' or 'to clear my house and mind so I can make the big decision'.

Big Peace Day 61: Burn Your House Down

'I think,' said Christopher Robin, 'that we ought to eat all of our provisions now, so we won't have much to carry.' – A A Milne

No, I don't mean you literally have to burn your house down. But I want you to imagine you went out for the evening and, while you were out, you lost all your possessions in the fire. No one was hurt – not family, not the pets. You've just lost material possessions – but all of them.

What are you devastated about losing?

What is irreplaceable?

Why?

Big Peace Day 62: Forgive

'To forgive is not just to be altruistic. It is the best form of self-interest. It is also a process that does not exclude hatred and anger. These emotions are all part of being human. You should never hate yourself for hating others who do terrible things: the depth of your love is shown by the extent of your anger.

However, when I talk of forgiveness I mean the belief that you can come out the other side a better person. A better person than the one being consumed by anger and hatred. Remaining in that state locks you in a state of victimhood, making you almost dependent on the perpetrator. If you can find it in yourself to forgive, then you are no longer chained to the perpetrator. You can move on, and you can even help the perpetrator to become a better person too'
– Desmond Tutu

OK, I understand that forgiveness is a big one, and I'm not suggesting that you tackle it in one day. But I would like you to contemplate the idea of forgiveness.

The study of forgiveness, once the preserve of theologians, has become the hottest field of research among clinical psychologists in America, where more than 1,000 studies on the subject have been published in the past five years. Much of the research focuses on the health benefits – both psychological and physical.

Evidence is mounting that holding on to grudges and bitterness results in long-term health problems. Forgiveness, on the other hand, offers numerous benefits, including:

❀ Lower blood pressure
❀ Stress reduction
❀ Less hostility
❀ Better anger management skills
❀ Lower heart rate
❀ Lower risk of alcohol or substance abuse
❀ Fewer depression symptoms
❀ Fewer anxiety symptoms
❀ Reduction in chronic pain
❀ More friendships
❀ Healthier relationships
❀ Greater religious or spiritual wellbeing
❀ Improved psychological wellbeing.

I'm not saying that forgiveness is easy; it's very much a process. I was incredibly inspired by the story of Jo Berry. Twenty-five years ago, she lost her father in the Brighton bombing. Rather than get angry, she chose to try to understand the bombers instead. So, several years later she made contact with the man responsible. Since then she and Patrick Magee, the IRA member who planted the bomb, have struck up a friendship as each struggles to understand the cause and effect of this devastating act of violence.

'I wanted to meet him as a human being rather than a demonized figure,' says Berry, whose father was the MP Sir Anthony Berry. 'I didn't want to save his soul; it was about me feeling better about myself.' She needed to understand what led Magee to such violence. 'It's about shared responsibility in terms of politics and history. Meeting him has helped me to heal.'

Forgiveness does help you heal. How? Research by the endocrinologist Dr Bruce McEwen of New York's Rockefeller University indicates that forgiveness could boost the immune system by reducing production of the 'stress hormone', cortisol. Cortisol can, if produced at high levels over a long period of time, cause physical harm.

But forgiveness is often easier said than done. Rage, anger and the idea of revenge can often feel better in the short term. In *Dare to Forgive*, psychiatrist Dr Edward Hallowell acknowledges the short-term pleasure of indulging your anger. He concedes that forgiveness never comes naturally. He describes anger like smoking a cigarette: short-term relief but with damaging long-term consequences.

So how do we forgive? Dr Everett Worthington, the psychologist and author of *Forgiveness and Reconciliation*, is not only a leading investigator of forgiveness but has also been on his own personal journey to forgiveness, too. In 1996, his aged mother was found beaten to death with a crowbar and baseball bat, after having been raped with a wine bottle.

Worthington describes a five-step process – albeit not an easy or quick one. He calls this process REACH.

1. R stands for *recall*. Recall the event that hurt you in as objective a way as possible. Do not see the person as evil, do not wallow in self-pity.

2. E stands for *empathize*. Step into the perpetrator's shoes. This is certainly not easy, but imagine the story the person would tell if they had to explain their actions.

3. A stands for *altruistic* – and giving the altruistic gift of forgiveness. Recall a time you messed up and then were forgiven – it made you feel better. Tell yourself you can rise above hurt and vengeance and give this gift.

4. C stands for *commit* to it. In Worthington's groups, his clients write a 'certificate of

forgiveness' – a letter of forgiveness to the
offender, written in their diary, in a poem or
song, however feels best for them. They also
tell a trusted friend what they have done.

5. H stands for *hold* – as in holding on to
    forgiveness. Another challenging step –
    memories of the event may occur and this
    requires a commitment not to dwell vengefully
    on the memory but to remind yourself that you
    are committed to forgiving.

Forgiveness does not have to mean forgetting about
the wrong done, or pretending it never happened. It's
about 'reaching' for a more productive state, and it
will make you healthier and happier in the long run.

Today, I just want you to ponder forgiveness
and visit www.theforgivenessproject.com and be
inspired by stories such as Jo Berry's. Just consider
the thought that forgiveness may be possible, and
perhaps ask yourself whether you want to take a first
step.

I'll leave you with the story of Eva Kor, one of the
stories featured on the website. Eva, at the age of ten
and along with her twin sister Miriam, was taken to
Auschwitz, where Dr Josef Mengele used them for
medical experiments. Both survived, but Miriam died
in 1993 when she developed cancer of the bladder
as a consequence of the experiments done on her as

a child. On 27 January 1995, at the 50th anniversary of the liberation of Auschwitz, Eva stood by the ruins of the gas chambers with her two grown-up children – and with Dr Munch, a Nazi who had been based in Auschwitz, and his children and grandchild. In their presence, Eva Kor signed a document of forgiveness. She writes of this moment: 'As I did that I felt a burden of pain was lifted from me. I was no longer in the grip of pain and hate; I was finally free. I believe with every fibre of my being that every human being has the right to live without the pain of the past. For most people there is a big obstacle to forgiveness because society expects revenge. It seems we need to honour our victims but I always wonder if my dead loved ones would want me to live with pain and anger until the end of my life.'

Big Peace Day 63: Embracing Odd Socks

'My definition of success is total self-acceptance. We can obtain all of the material possessions we desire quite easily; however, attempting to change our deepest thoughts and learning to love ourselves is a monumental challenge. We may achieve success in our business lives but it never quite means as much if we do not feel good inside. Once we feel good about ourselves inside we can genuinely lend ourselves to others.' – Victor Frankl

It's been a heavy week. So I want to end on a lighter note and the idea that the road to inner peace is far more about self-acceptance than self-improvement. Most of my friends are all wonderfully organized and tidy. For years, I have looked at their lives, taken notes, thought 'that is so impressive' and devised a constantly growing to-do list – 'must be more organized, must be tidier, must have matching socks'. And I never, ever managed it. All my to-do list did was keep me running, always out of breath, always trying and failing to reach the standards I set myself. What would happen if I tore it up, I pondered?

So I wrote my ultimate list: all the things I felt I 'should' do to be shiny and perfect – from wearing matching knickers and bras to creating a computer database of all my addresses. Then I ripped it up and waited for chaos to ensue. But it didn't. Everything remained the same, except that I got more relaxed. When I stopped trying to be a tidy/organized/all-my-addresses-in-one-place sort of person, I let go of this huge weight of guilt. Yes, my son and I wear odd socks most of the time, but I no longer fret about it.

I have realized that there are some details in life that simply don't matter to me. Over the last ten years, I have learned the hard way that it really is important for my sanity to have my basic bill-paying/food-buying/business organizational systems in place. But matching bras, knickers and socks? I actually don't care. But I thought I should.

When you start to let go of those 'shoulds', there is a lot less noise in your head, which leaves you free to, well, figure out what you really do want to do with your time and energy.

A quick question: What list of 'shoulds' could you let go of today?

Week 10

Who Loves Ya, Baby?

'Come out of the circle of time, and into the circle of love.' – **Rumi**

The better your relationships, the happier and more peaceful your life will be. As we've already heard in Week 8, isolation makes us miserable and connecting with other people makes us happy.

To create wonderful relationships, you need to brush up on your 'connection' skills. I have been coaching for ten years now, and before that was a journalist, so I have spent years watching and listening to those who do and do not connect with others well. I have noticed that people who connect beautifully have three specific skills and attributes:

1. listening
2. acknowledging
3. being authentic.

People who connect with others brilliantly listen the most. Dale Carnegie wrote the cult classic *How to Win Friends and Influence People* and shared an anecdote about how he sat next to a scientist at an event. Carnegie just kept asking him questions and got the scientist to open up. Whenever there was a lull in the conversation, Carnegie would ask another question. At the end of the event, the scientist went up to his host and proclaimed that Carnegie was the most interesting man he'd ever met! Carnegie writes: 'You can make more friends in two months by becoming really interested in other people than you can in two years by trying to get other people interested in you. Which is just another way of saying that the way to make a friend is to be one.'

Another powerful way to connect to others is to acknowledge who they are versus what they do. If you listen for and point out their special gifts, traits or talents, you can affect them in an incredibly positive way. Praising what someone has done is good, but that can often make people feel they have to 'do' to be valuable in the world. When someone points out what is great about you, it immediately lowers those 'I'm not good enough' defences. It's also great for you, because when you are constantly focusing and looking for what is good about someone (rather than what's bad), it makes you a wonderful person to be around and someone everyone wants to connect to. Think about the most judgemental people you know. Do you really want to spend a lot of time with them?

Lastly, be authentic – tell the truth about yourself. There is nothing so attractive as someone who is comfortable in their own skin with nothing to prove. When you are self-secure, others feel safe around you. When you accept your humanness, faults as well as talents, then others feel they can drop their façades and connect on a deeper level. People 'get' when you're not trying to prove anything to yourself or others.

When you can be truly honest about your challenges as well as your successes, when you can acknowledge others for who they are versus what they do, and by really listening to others, you will feel supported, loved and respected for who you really are. And the scientists are right: that makes you feel really happy.

This is going to be a lovely week.

Big Peace Day 64: Prime Time

'If you would be loved, love and be lovable.'
– Benjamin Franklin

Today I want to talk about what I call 'mother-love', or
what British psychiatrist John Bowlby called 'attachment
theory'. This theory explores the three attachment styles
formed early in life as a result of how we have interacted
with our mothers or primary caregivers.

Bowlby discovered that a child who built up
trust in those closest to her as sources of comfort
developed a sense that the world is a safe place. But
those babies who failed to find comfort, and felt
alone rather than secure, grew up believing that the
world and others couldn't be trusted.

A child can react to this second scenario in two
ways – with an 'anxious' attachment style or an
'avoidant' attachment style. Those with an anxious
attachment style desperately try to become close to
people, attempting to attract their attention and gain
their protection. They are needy for other people's
love, and even when they are in a loving relationship,
they fear they might lose it.

Those with an 'avoidant' attachment style give
up on others and develop a steely self-reliance. They
don't believe that others can help when they need

it. As an adult, they might be described as commit-phobes, they may prefer to work alone and they distrust most people.

'Emotionally secure' is the tag given to those whose early care-giving was responsive and comforting – for those who grew up feeling there was someone there for them when they were upset. They built a foundation of trust that the key people would be there for them when needed. As adults, these people are curious, confident with high self-esteem – and happier romantic relationships.

In her brilliant book *The Plastic Mind*, award-winning *Newsweek* columnist Sharon Bagley reports on pioneering experiments in neuroplasticity (the brain's potential to change). Her chapter called 'Blaming Mom? Rewired for Compassion' is life-changing for the individual and has profound implications for the way we live our lives. She reports on Professor Phillip Shaver, a social and personality psychologist who set out to discover if Bowlby's attachment styles were set in stone. Shaver used a technique called 'priming' where volunteers were subliminally exposed to words associated with emotional security – such as 'hug', 'closeness', 'love', 'support' – and discovered that priming enabled people to become emotionally stable – even those who were extremely anxious or avoidant.

Not only that, but as part of Shaver's research programme, volunteers who were primed with an attachment-security story, memory or words seemed to show more compassion and loving kindness towards others – even if it meant picking up a tarantula on their behalf. Yes, you read that right.

In one experiment, Shaver examined whether enhancing attachment security would change not only how people said they felt and thought – but how they acted.

In this experiment, volunteers were asked to take a test to assess their attachment style – anxious, avoidant or stable – and then were asked to take part in an experiment where a young woman had been randomly assigned to perform unpleasant tasks such as looking at gory photographs, petting a rat and letting cockroaches and a tarantula climb up her arm. The volunteers were asked to watch as she performed these tasks. The volunteers were told that the woman was a student like themselves and was in the next room being filmed. In reality, it was a pre-recorded film and the 'volunteer' was one of the researchers – called Liat. The volunteers were asked to rate their emotional reactions as to how much compassion, personal distress, sympathy, tenderness and discomfort they felt for their fellow 'student', Liat.

Liat completed several of the unpleasant tasks, but when she got to handling the tarantula, feigned refusal. The experimenter 'switched off' the camera and, having 'talked' to Liat in the next room, told the volunteers that the study could not continue unless someone else would pet the tarantula – and would they do it?

Shaver and his team wanted to see if the volunteers would act on their feelings of compassion. Those who were 'avoidant' in style showed lower levels of compassion and were less willing to help. Those with an 'anxious' attachment style were very distressed while watching, but were no more willing to help. But when those with either an avoidant or anxious style were subliminally primed with the name of someone they had said they could rely on for emotional support, the results were incredibly different. Not only did volunteers report higher levels of compassion, but they would also actually agree to take Liat's place to relieve her distress.

This led Shaver to conclude: 'Those who got the security prime were significantly more compassionate. They felt more inclined to help the suffering woman. This makes it seem that if you can make a person feel more secure, they will have a greater capacity to feel for someone who is suffering, and will be moved to do something about it. Making a person feel more secure had this beneficial effect independent of their inherent avoidance or anxiety. It worked on everyone.'

Today, let's prime you up with love. Create your three ultimate love memories. Recall someone who loved you, loves you and who is there for you, has supported you, hugged and cared for you when you needed them to be there for you. Recall the memory and visualize it vividly. Write down the three memories in vivid detail: Where are you, what are they wearing, what are they saying, how does that make you feel? Give each memory a short-hand name, such as 'Ailsa – by the lake', 'Grace on our walk', 'Dad coming home'.

A useful trick is, while you're doing this, press your index finger and thumb together. This is a tool used by practitioners of Neuro-Linguistic Programming. It links the feeling of being loved with a physical sensation. Keep repeating this exercise and then, later, see if simply pressing your fingers together will help trigger the feeling of being loved.

Big Peace Day 65: Love Yourself, Why Don't You?

'All the strength you need to achieve anything is within you. Don't wait for a light to appear at the end of the tunnel, stride down there ... and light the bloody thing yourself.' – **Sara Anderson**

Loving yourself? Ah, that old chestnut. So many of the great self-development teachers tell us that the key to inner peace is loving ourselves. And I agree. What do you think would happen if you could become your biggest fan instead of your harshest critic?

I suspect we've all got a story of how we got to this place. We've been working with lots of techniques in this book to change that story. Today, I want you to put your money where your mouth is. I want to take you completely out of your comfort zone as you create three simple, practical practices that scream SELF-ADORATION. Make them small and doable, BUT adoring.

Ah, has your mind gone completely blank?

Start here: Think of your best friend – and what you would do for him/her to show your adoration? Buy a favourite CD? Tickets for a favourite show? A long lunch? Flowers? A subscription to a favourite magazine? Look after the kids while he or she goes to the spa/footie match?

The trick is to come up with a massive long list so you can visit it daily and create a daily dose of adoration. Yes, yes, I can feel your resistance. The whole 'deserving' issue might come up, not enough time, energy, inspiration … blah, blah, blah. But push through that resistance. Start treating yourself like you are adored and, today, act your way into a new way of being.

Big Peace Day 66: Listen to Some Loving Words

'Love cures people – both the ones who give it and the ones who receive it.' – Dr Karl Menninger

Lovely homework today: get a person who loves you to sit you down and spend five minutes explaining why you are fantastic, wonderful and loved exactly how you are right now.

Big Peace Day 67: Open Your Heart

'Honey, if I weren't rich, would you still love me?'
  'Of course I'd love you – I'd miss you, but I'd love
you ...' – as told by Norman Cousins

Dr Dean Ornish, a pioneer cardiologist and bestselling author of *Reversing Heart Disease*, 'achieved the impossible' by creating a programme and scientific proof that heart disease could be halted and even reversed by changing your lifestyle.

As well as encouraging his patients to make healthier lifestyle choices such as changing to a healthier diet, exercising and stopping smoking, a main part of Ornish's programme was getting his patients to reconnect with loved ones and to decrease loneliness. He bases the programme on a body of scientific evidence that shows that, be it rabbits, monkeys or men, intimacy and social support can be healing.

Noticing several similar emotional characteristics in his heart patients, Ornish suggests that emotions such as self-involvement, hostility and cynicism predispose us to heart disease. But they are simply the *symptoms*. The real underlying problem, he says, is isolation:

'When someone feels isolated and alone, then his focus is on himself: 'I feel alone, I am lacking, if only I had ..., then I'd be happy.' Which sets up a vicious cycle, says Ornish, that a person would become compulsively driven to achieve this thing only to find it didn't make them happy. Which leads to disappointment and disillusionment– which then leads to cynicism.

The real paradox is that we try to set ourselves apart from other people as a way of trying to become more intimate with them: 'Look at me – I'm special! I'm worthy of your attention and respect! Love me!' But what does it mean to be special? To be special means to be different. To be set apart from other people – so the irony is that we set ourselves apart and further isolate ourselves in a futile attempt to feel reconnected and re-empowered.'

Ornish created a five-step process to reconnect and communicate with others. Today, try out his communication process:

❉ *Step 1: Identify What You Are Feeling*
Sounds easy, but be careful that your thoughts don't masquerade as feelings – for example, the feeling 'I'm angry' versus the thought 'You're wrong', or the feeling 'I'm worried' versus the thought: 'You're late.'

❀ *Step 2: Express What You Are Feeling*
Express how you feel, but not as a judgement or
criticism. Be wary of statements like 'You should ...'
'You always...' 'You never ...'

❀ *Step 3: Listen Actively with Empathy and*
   Compassion
Try to listen to what the other person is really
saying. Try to step into the other person's shoes. Try
to really see their point of view.

❀ *Step 4: Acknowledge What the Other Person Is*
   Saying
Express that you understand what the other person
is saying or what you think they're saying: 'So
you're feeling very frustrated and angry that I'm
late?'

Big Peace Day 68: Make a Gratitude Visit

*The best and most beautiful things in the world
cannot be seen or even touched – they must be felt
with the heart.'* – **Helen Keller**

Yesterday we were learning how important
connection with our fellow human beings is, and we
learned some fantastic communication skills. Today

we're going to use a super-boosting technique that is about connecting on a profound level and that will affect your feelings of wellbeing for weeks.

Today, initiate a 'gratitude visit'. That means writing a testimonial thanking a teacher, friend or grandparent – anyone to whom you owe a debt of gratitude – and then visiting them to read them the letter of appreciation. It will not only make them feel fantastic, it's scientifically proven to make you happier, too. Research shows that people who do this just once are measurably happier and less depressed even a month later.

Today, write that letter of gratitude to someone who has moved or affected your life in a positive way, and make an appointment to go and visit them.

Big Peace Day 69: Stop Thinking about Yourself

'Unless someone like you cares a whole awful lot, nothing is going to get better. It's not.' – **Dr Seuss**

Studies have shown that helping others gives us a 'helper's high' – a physical and emotional sensation of euphoria that lasts for days or even weeks.

Not only that, but the more you do good, the more optimistic you will become, you'll have more energy, better perceived health, better weight control and a greater sense of relaxation – as well as a stronger immune system.

Today – do a good deed for someone. And notice how it makes you feel.

Big Peace Day 70: How to Get On with Anyone

'To get others to come into our ways of thinking, we must go over to theirs; and it is necessary to follow in order to lead.' – **William Hazlitt**

One of the biggest peace-givers (and also peace-robbers) around is – other people! Although it might actually not be possible to get on with other people all the time, there are a couple of techniques that you can learn that will help you if you find yourself constantly fighting with your in-laws, your boss or someone significant – or even someone insignificant.

Today, think about someone you can't stand. Now, for five minutes, step into the other person's shoes and see life through their eyes. Get a sheet of paper and write quickly and without thinking too hard: What does X believe about these ten issues: work/motherhood/parenting/love/money/life/sex/relationships/housework/health?

Once you've written a phrase or sentence for each, write down *why* you think X believes these things. Is it the way they were brought up? The more you understand where they're coming from, the easier it will be to see them as human beings rather than some kind of monster/enemy. If you can understand and then accept that this is simply the way they see the world, and nothing to do with a personal attack on you, you can stop being defensive.

Next, decide to give up your painful story. If you're struggling with someone, it's often because you are telling or retelling some kind of 'painful story'. By telling this story, we label and judge someone. Then we spend our time constantly searching for evidence to support this view of them. You may have made a decision that someone is 'nice but dim' or 'controlling and manipulative', 'cold and competitive'. So try this exercise.

First, define in two adjectives how you would describe this other person. Now ask yourself which painful story these adjectives refer back to. For example, the time when your mother-in-law turned up and the first thing she did was put on her rubber gloves and clean your kitchen – and you decided she was controlling and judgemental. Now ask yourself if you'd be willing to start looking for a new story to tell. Ask yourself what two new, positive adjectives you could find to describe your mother-in-law. For example, supportive and helpful. You may not be able to change the other person, but you can change the way you see them and the stories you tell yourself about them in your head.

Week 11

What Else?

'Ultimately, what we are looking to is the deepest connection within ourselves. As we get more connected to that, we begin to feel in harmony with other people and with the rest of the world.'

– Shakti Gawain

We've covered a lot of exercises so far in the Big Peace process. Why? Because I feel that we will all have different entry methods into The Big Peace. Whereas visualization will work for some, hypnotherapy or life coaching might work for others.

If it were up to me, I'd tell you all to get a dog. My beautiful cocker spaniel Oscar – although very smelly – brings me so much peace and unconditional love, and gets me out walking in the beautiful countryside every day. Every time I take Oscar out, my body gets flooded with feel-good endorphins (see Day 39); I feel calm, at peace and loved up! It brings me 'thinner peace' too! I joined a gym and put on three pounds, but I have lost almost two stone just getting out with Oscar every day.

Science backs me up, too. In a recent review of several scientific studies, dog owners were found to be less stressed – and physically and psychologically healthier.

But I understand that you may not all be dog-lovers. So in Week 11 I want you to try some other scientifically proven new and ancient methods that are guaranteed to make you feel peaceful – well, if you make them part of your daily Big Peace practice, that is. Plus a few of my own personal favourites.

The first few exercises are about focusing inward, which will allow you to be very clear for the last few exercises – which are about what you wish to spend your energy and time on.

We are coming to the end of our 90-day journey together. I could have given these exercises to you at the beginning of our journey together, but I'm hoping that all the work you've done will enable you to have got some obstacles to peace out of the way first. You can now enjoy these techniques to the full. Some are very simple, but their effects are profound.

Enjoy.

Big Peace Day 71: Be a Child

'I did not come to yoga to stretch. I came to live.'
— Maya Breuer

Today try the yoga pose known as 'The Child'.

Yoga is an ancient system that originated in India and has been around for 5,000 years, so why is it becoming increasingly popular now?

Viv Alves, founder of yoga company Warrior at Work, and my very own yoga teacher, says: 'Stress-related illnesses are rampant these days. People are feeling increasingly isolated as our communities break down and we are slowly becoming disillusioned with the materialistic "I'm all right, Jack" culture. Practising yoga helps people to feel calm, at peace and at one with their fellow human beings – and essentially gives you a practical way to connect to yourself. It's a holistic antidote for many of today's challenges.'

Yoga can also work wonders on your body. Incorporating mind, breath and body in a combination of movements called *asanas*, it keeps muscles and ligaments strong and supple. It can improve areas such as the stomach, bottom and thighs, while the increased blood flow can assist organ efficiency and aid digestion – giving you what practitioners call 'an internal workout'.

But Viv is very sceptical of introducing yoga as some kind of Indian keep-fit idea: 'Derived from the Sanskrit word for union, yoga works both on the body and the mind. Every aspect of yoga is holistic. Yes, you will tone up but the benefits of yoga are as much spiritual as they are physical.'

Yoga can also greatly improve your health. Recent research has shown that asthma sufferers reported fewer attacks and less frequent use of medication within just two weeks of taking up yoga. A study at Harvard University Medical School also found that yoga breathing can lower blood pressure and decrease anxiety. Yoga is also generally known to relieve conditions such as back pain, allergies, headaches, insomnia and depression.

For inner peace, Viv recommends we try The Child's Pose, which has us folding ourselves forward into a foetal position:

Kneel on your heels with the tops of your feet flat on the floor. Slowly lower your head down onto the floor, lengthening the spine away from the hips, aiming to keep your bottom on your heels. If your bottom lifts, support your head with a blanket or make fists with your hands to rest your head on.

Breathe deeply and focus on inhaling – expanding your chest and ribcage. When exhaling, lengthen your spine vertebra by vertebra – feeling the hips drawing to the floor, drawn down by gravity. Stay and breathe for as long as you wish.

Focus on the thought: 'I can trust my inner self, all that I need is already here. I accept who and what I am and I am at peace.'

Big Peace Day 72: Develop Life's Most Important Skill

'Meditation is not a way to enlightenment,
Nor is it a method of achieving anything at all.
It is peace itself.
It is the actualization of wisdom,
The ultimate truth of the oneness of all things.' – Dogen

In *Happiness, A Guide to Developing Life's Most Important Skill*, written by Buddhist monk Matthieu Ricard (sometimes called 'the happiest man in the world'), Ricard argues that inner peace is not just an emotion but a skill that can be developed. Biochemist-turned-Buddhist monk Matthieu Ricard says we can train our minds in habits of wellbeing, to generate a true sense of serenity and fulfilment:

'We willingly spend dozens of years in school, then go on to college or professional training for several more; we work out at the gym to stay healthy; we spend a lot of time enhancing our comfort, our wealth, our social status. We put a great deal into all this, and yet we do little to improve the inner condition that determines the very quality of our lives.'

There has been a mountain of research that shows that meditation – training the mind on the development of constructive emotions – can work remarkably well to give us a sense of inner calm.

But new research conducted with brain imaging on the Buddhist loving-kindness meditation is also showing that compassion meditation lights up the part of the brain that correlates with people's well-being and positive emotions like joy and enthusiasm. This corroborates the research that shows that the most altruistic members of a population are also those who are the most satisfied with life.

Richard Davidson, director of the study and Professor of Psychiatry and Psychology at the University of Wisconsin at Madison monitored 16 Buddhist monks who had practised about 10,000 hours of meditation.

Using brain-imaging techniques, the researchers found that brain activity while meditating on compassion was especially high in the left prefrontal lobe (the Big Peace place) and swamped activity in the right prefrontal lobe, where negative emotions and anxiety show up. This was something that had never been seen as being caused purely by mental activity alone.

Obviously, we're not all Buddhist monks with 10,000 hours of meditation practice behind us, but another study conducted by Davidson has shown that three months of meditation training with ordinary mortals also significantly shifted activity in their brains from right to left. Meditation also boosted the control group's immune system, showing that meditation make us less stressed and healthier.

Today, we're going to try a compassion-meditation exercise from *Happiness, A Guide to Developing Life's Most Important Skill* by Matthieu Ricard.

Begin by generating a powerful feeling of warmth, loving kindness and compassion for all beings. Then imagine those who are enduring suffering similar to or worse than your own. As you breathe out, visualize that you are sending them all your happiness, vitality, good fortune, health and so on, on your breath in the form of cool, white, luminous nectar. Picture them fully absorbing the nectar, which soothes their pain and fulfils their aspirations. If their life is in danger of being cut short, imagine that it has been prolonged; if they are sick, imagine that they are healed; if they are poor and helpless, imagine that they have obtained what they need; if they are unhappy, that they have become full of joy.

When you inhale, visualize your heart as a bright luminous sphere. Imagine that you are taking upon yourself, in the form of a grey cloud, the disease, confusion and mental toxins of these people, which disappears into the white light of your heart without leaving any trace. This will transform both your own suffering and that of others. There is no sense that you are being burdened by them. When you are taking upon yourself and dissolving their sufferings, feel a great happiness, without attachment or clinging.

You can imagine that your body is duplicating itself in countless forms that travel throughout the universe, transforming itself into clothing for those who are cold, food for the famished, or shelter for the homeless.

Matthieu Richard says, 'This visualization is a powerful means to develop benevolence and compassion. It can be carried out any time and during your day-to-day activities. It does not require you to neglect your own well-being; instead it allows you to adjust your reaction to unavoidable suffering by assigning new value to it. In fact, identifying clearly your own aspiration to well-being is the first step towards feeling genuine empathy for others' suffering. Furthermore, this attitude significantly increases your enthusiasm and readiness to work for the good of others.'

Big Peace Day 73: Breathe into Your Belly

'I've got to keep breathing. It'll be my worst business mistake if I don't.' – Steve Martin

OK, this is an incredibly simple technique that can be done anywhere, any time.

Take three breaths right into your belly – expand not only your chest but breathe right into your belly until it expands.

When we are feeling anxious and the flight-or-fight stress response is triggered, our breathing becomes irregular and shallow. Deep breathing into the belly, on the other hand, physiologically switches off the flight-or-fight response. This will decrease your heart rate, metabolic rate and blood sugar levels, relieve muscle tension and stress – and give you an instant sense of calm.

Today, practise your belly breaths.

Or try breathing from your heart. I have recently discovered an amazing little machine called the emWave Personal Stress Reliever – an interactive stress-relief system that reads your heart rhythms through a thumb or ear sensor and gives immediate feedback through changing-coloured lights and sound.

emWave technology has been developed by the Heartmath organisation, which has conducted intensive scientific research that shows that when you intentionally shift to a positive emotion, heart rhythms immediately change. This shift in heart rhythms creates a favourable cascade of neural, hormonal and biochemical events that benefit the entire body. The effects are both immediate and long lasting. It is a brilliant and fun tool to show you visually and by listening to the changing tones emanating from your emWave that you are inhabiting your Big Peace place.

Plug yourself into your emWave machine and focus on your heart and imagine breathing in and out from your heart. And just see what happens. Magic!

Big Peace Day 74: Visualize Your Big Peace

'If you can imagine it, you can achieve it; if you can dream it, you can become it.' – **William Arthur Ward**

We've been doing lots of visualizing over the last few weeks. Why? Because it works. Science is showing that the mind cannot tell the difference between real and imagined.

The scientists don't know exactly how it works, says Dr David Hamilton, author of *How Your Mind Can Heal Your Body*. The theory is that different thoughts and mental states release hormones that can dramatically accelerate or stop muscle growth, fire up or slow down your metabolism, even switching genes on and off to tip the genetic balance towards healing.

In Hamilton's book, he lists case history after case history of those who have healed themselves through visualization – using it for everything from fighting cancer to losing weight.

Hamilton suggests we visualize three times a day or more.

Try this meditation for inner peace:

Imagine a ball of soft green, pink or white light in the centre of your brain or heart, or see it like a little candle flame. This represents your inner peace and happiness. Note its size.

Now imagine a dial and turn it up. As you do this, see the light get bigger and bigger and brighter. Mentally affirm that it is a symbol of your inner strength, peace and happiness.

Continue to turn the dial and watch the light get bigger and brighter. See it expand right out of your head or heart and throughout your entire body. See the light flow through your arteries and your veins, though your heart and your internal organs. Imagine it tickling your cells and organs and see them smile. See it flow over your skin and imagine your skin cells smiling. See yourself surrounded by this powerful light and mentally affirm that your power and peace and happiness are great.

Big Peace Day 75: The Cake of Life

'The key to keeping your balance is knowing when you've lost it.' – **Anonymous**

Today try one of the most popular life-coaching exercises ever. Known by most as the 'wheel of life' exercise, I call it the cake of life. It's a brilliant exercise to create balance and peace in your life.

Draw a circle that represents your 'cake of life'.
Now draw lines to separate it into eight slices of
cake. Name each piece of cake:

1. relationship
2. health
3. money
4. environment
5. friends
6. work
7. me-time
8. family.

Now, give each slice a score out of 10 (10 being
feeling fantastic and fulfilled). Then, starting with
the piece of cake with the lowest score, for the
next seven days concentrate on raising your score
by two points.

For example, if you need to spend more time with
your partner, book a date night to raise that score.
If you need to look at your cash situation, book an
appointment with a financial advisor. Once one week
is over, choose the piece of cake with the next-lowest
score and spend the next seven days focusing on that
piece. Keep working on your cake until each slice
has a score of 8/10 or over.

Big Peace Day 76: Apply the 80/20 Rule to Inner Peace

'Our life is frittered away by detail ... simplify, simplify.' – Henry David Thoreau

Vilfredo Pareto was an economist born in 1848 who created what is popularly known as 'the 80/20 rule'. This says that 80 per cent of consequences flow from 20 per cent of causes. Put another way, 80 per cent of results come from 20 per cent of our efforts and time. It is quite a radical idea to get your head around, but if you work with this it can have a far-reaching and massive impact on your life – especially if you apply this principle to your inner peace.

Today, look at your life and ask yourself these two questions:

❀ Which 20 per cent of sources are causing 80 per cent of my problems and unhappiness? For example, is your relationship with your boss draining your energy? Is a friend/relative or spouse creating 80 per cent of your problems?

❀ Which 20 per cent of sources are resulting in 80 per cent of feeling peaceful and calm?

Once you've answered these two questions, take a long hard look and create a list of actions that you can take to deal with the people/things/events from the first and focus your energy on the people/things/events in the second.

Big Peace Day 77: What's Your Priority for Peace?

'Set peace of mind as your highest goal, and organize your life around it.' – **Brian Tracy**

There is a wonderful coach, whom I love, called Talane Miedaner, author of *Coach Yourself to Success*. She has taught me a brilliant tool for focusing on what is important to me.

I had just launched a new business project, was a new mum and I never, ever seemed to have enough time to do everything that just needed to be done. I was constantly stressed, and any semblance of inner peace had gone.

'You've forgotten what really matters most,' Talane said to me.

She told me to ask myself these three questions every morning before I got stuck into my day:

❀ What is important about today?
❀ What must I get done today?
❀ What is important about my future?

I still ask these questions almost every day. It helps me get my life priorities in order.

What is important about today? Often the most important part of my day is spending time with my son.

What must I get done today? This question focuses me and stops me stressing out about things that are simply not important. Sometimes I have to go to a meeting or coach a client, but usually there are only one or two 'musts'.

The question about the future keeps me centred in the present. If I didn't ask this question, my books or new projects wouldn't ever get started, so it encourages me to take action now.

Week 12

Who Are You *Not* to Be?

'Our deepest fear is not that we are inadequate. Our deepest fear is that we are powerful beyond measure. It is our light, not our darkness, that most frightens us. We ask ourselves, who am I to be brilliant, gorgeous, talented and fabulous?

'Actually, who are you not to be?

'You are a child of God. Your playing small doesn't serve the world. There's nothing enlightened about shrinking so that other people won't feel insecure around you.

'We were born to make and manifest the glory of God that is within us. It's not just in some of us; it's in everyone. And as we let our own light shine, we unconsciously give other people permission to do the same. As we are liberated from our own fear, our presence automatically liberates others'

– **Marianne Williamson, *A Return to Love***

It's the last week (well, 12 days) of our 90-day Big Peace course.

How are you feeling?

I thought I'd end the programme with inspiration from one of my favourite authors, Marianne Williamson, who wrote the book *A Return to Love*, among others.

I went to a talk she gave in London a few years ago and she wryly talked about the angry young woman she used to be when she embarked on her marches for peace in the 1960s.

Finally, she talked about the shift she made from 'fighting for peace' to 'being peace', and she quoted Gandhi: 'Be the change you want to see in the world,' she encouraged us.

'When we stop fighting for peace out there and start creating peace "in here", miracles happen,' she said.

I do love a miracle, so I went back home and pondered:

- ✿ How can I BE more peaceful?
- ✿ How can I stop focusing on the rollercoaster of events out there that send me into a tailspin and keep focused on my own internal state?
- ✿ How can I stay loving and kind when I want to blame, point fingers and run for the hills?

🌸 If I want to live a life without war, how can I stop fighting in my own everyday life?

🌸 If I want a life of peace, how can I 'be' that on a daily basis?

I know writing and researching this book and starting this journey have helped me answer some of those questions. I hope that reading it has helped you, too.

Over the next 12 days I just want to ask you 12 simple questions – one per day – which will hopefully help you review what has worked and inspire you to create your very own Big Peace practice.

Big Peace Day 78: Reviewing Week 1 - Anything Changed?

'You've taken your first step into a larger world.'
— Ben Kenobi to Luke Skywalker in Star Wars

Today, book 15 minutes out of your day and do the thought bubble exercises. Watch as your thoughts arise and write them down one by one. Today – what do you notice? What do you observe? Did you find it easier today than you did 12 weeks ago? Or was it harder? Were thoughts more of the same or different?

Are your needs still driving you or did you get help to get those needs met?

Did you create a needs-fulfilment project – how did that go? What worked? What didn't?

Big Peace Day 79: Reviewing Week 2 - Do You Know Who You Want to Be?

'I would rather be a superb meteor, every atom of me in magnificent glow, than a sleepy and permanent planet. The proper function of a man is to live, not to exist.' – Jack London

What new belief did you adopt in Week 2? What evidence did you start to build about a new way of seeing yourself and the world? What new rules of living did you create? What old thoughts did you begin to question?

What is working for you? Ten weeks on, what have you discovered about what you believe about yourself – what works and what doesn't?

Big Peace Day 80: Reviewing Week 3 - Have You Been Braver?

'I was taught bravery and that has influenced me.'
– Helen Mirren

It's easier to be braver with your Inner Coach by your side. Has s/he been by your side? Have you been tuned in to Big Peace radio? Is your little Inner Pessimist child growing up more secure now s/he has a new nurturing influence in life?

How fast do you notice when your Inner Pessimist is in charge? What have you found is the best technique to leap from fear to love?

Big Peace Day 81: Reviewing Week 4 - Have You Got a New Story?

'Your pain is the breaking of the shell that encloses your understanding.' – Kahlil Gibran

Are you transforming any old, unsupportive stories that you have been telling yourself? What happens when you notice that you're telling the old story? What helps you to make a big leap in thinking and focus on a Big Peace thought? What doesn't work? If you were to fine-tune your technique, what could you do differently?

Big Peace Day 82: Reviewing Week 5 - What Do You Really Want?

'Twenty years from now you will be more disappointed by the things you didn't do than by the ones you did do. So throw off the bowlines. Sail away from the safe harbor. Catch the trade winds in your sails. Explore. Dream. Discover.' – **Mark Twain**

Have you discovered what gives you joy? Have you found your flow and your golden glow? What is it like to live an internally-driven life rather than an externally-driven one? What feels fantastic? What are you loving doing? What isn't working so well? What's in the way of your flow? What do you need to do or be differently to feel fulfilled, to find your purpose, to feel at peace?

Big Peace Day 83: Reviewing Week 6 - Are You Happy Now?

'Happiness is inward and not outward; and so it does not depend on what we have, but on what we are.'
– **Henry Van Dyke**

Did you let go of your 'I'll be happy when …' goals? Are you happy now? What's making you happy? If not, what thought is in the way of your happiness? What are you grateful for – what and who do you love? And what is working for you on a daily basis? Why do you think it's working?

Big Peace Day 84: Reviewing Week 7 - How Slow Can You Go?

'Be not afraid of growing slowly, be afraid of standing still.' – **Chinese proverb**

How slow did you go? How slow can you go? Did it feel good? Or just too scary? What's the perfect speed for you? What's too fast? What's too slow? How many hours' sleep do you need to feel 'done'? What's best done slow?

Big Peace Day 85: Reviewing Week 8 - Did You Cry?

'Hearts will never be practical until they are made unbreakable.' – **The Wizard of Oz**

What does it feel like to let go? Horrible? Liberating? What has happened to you and your life since you wrote it down and out? Nothing? Has anything changed? Have you noticed any difference? If yes, what?

Big Peace Day 86: Reviewing Week 9 - Are You Letting Go?

'People cannot discover new oceans until they lose sight of the shore.' – André Gide

Have you burnt your house down, acknowledged you're dying and considered forgiving someone? It was a big week in Week 9. Did you de-junk your house? Your life? What did you manage to let go of? What feels good? What doesn't? Is there anything else you need to let go of?

Big Peace Day 87: Reviewing Week 10 - Who Do You Love?

'If you want others to be happy, practise compassion. If you want to be happy, practise compassion.'
– Dalai Lama

Do you love yourself? Who else do you love? Do they love you? What about everyone else? Can you make some space on your couch for those who get on your nerves? Is love really the answer? If not, what is?

Big Peace Day 88: Reviewing Week 11 - What Else?

'Peace is not merely a distant goal that we seek but a means by which we arrive at that goal.'

– Martin Luther King

In Week 11, there were scientifically proven methods to make you feel calmer and more peaceful – which was your favourite? Which did you resist? Is there any method that you could include in your Big Peace practice? Why did it work for you?

Big Peace Day 89: Reviewing Week 12 - What Has Worked for You?

'Until one is committed there is hesitancy, the chance to draw back, always ineffectiveness.' – Goethe

What tools over the last 90 days have really worked for you? If you were to create a simple, do-able, everyday Big Peace practice, what would it consist of? What absolutely under no circumstances will ever work for you? What might work with a little more investigation? What can you commit to making part of your life?

Big Peace Day 90: Let's Start, But Slowly

'Happiness does not come automatically. It is not a gift that good fortune bestows upon us and a reversal of fortune takes back. It depends on us alone. One does not become happy overnight, but with patient labor, day after day. Happiness is constructed, and that requires effort and time. In order to become happy, we have to learn how to change ourselves.'

– Luca and Francesco Cavalli-Sforza

OK, we're done. I've given you everything I've got on how to grow the Big Peace in the garden of your mind. I'm not saying that I haven't missed anything or that this is THE one and only way. But right here, right now, these are the best tools I have found to create more peace in our lives. They will only work, however, if you use them.

Today, choose which tools and techniques you are going to use to create your Big Peace practice. Start with the easiest one(s). Choose a maximum of four practices that you can use every day. Build confidence about creating a sustainable practice by starting modestly. Don't promise that you're going to meditate eight hours a day – and thereby prove to yourself that, 'You see, I knew this wouldn't work for me.' Start with five minutes a day.

Changes in the brain and behaviour can take place in a surprisingly short space of time. But I'd encourage you to set a 90-day 'exercise' programme. As Dr David Hamilton says,

'Studies show that the more we do the same thing, or think the same thought, the more the changes occur in the brain, so changes will be more established after 90 days than, say, 21 or 30 days. Areas of the brain related to what we are doing or what we are thinking expand and contract, through neuroplasticity, as we keep doing or thinking something or as we stop it.'

The trick is to keep going and not stop. Studies at Harvard University have shown extensive brain changes in volunteers playing piano for two hours a day on five consecutive days. But what is not always reported is that the study also found that if they stopped for two days and then started again, the areas of the brain that had grown had begun to shrink again, and it took a couple of days to get back to where they had been before they stopped.

'Thinking positively, visualizing, thinking loving and compassionate thoughts for 90 days make a significant impact upon our brains in a beneficial way that will lead to a greater feeling of mental and emotional wellbeing. These types of thoughts will lead to measurable changes in the prefrontal cortex, in a similar (although not identical) way to meditation,' says Dr Hamilton.

Good luck, farewell, and may the force be with you!

Further Reading and Resources

Vivienne Alves – www.warrioratwork.com: Yoga for inner strength and peace

Martha Beck, *Steering by Starlight* (Piatkus, 2008)
   http://www.marthabeck.com/ – Resources and inspiration from my favourite life coach

Sharon Begley, *The Plastic Mind* (Constable, 2009)

William Bloom, *The Endorphin Effect* (Piatkus, 2001)

Will Bowen, *A Complaint Free World: How to Stop Complaining and Start Enjoying the Life You Always Wanted* (Doubleday, 2007)

Dale Carnegie, *How to Win Friends and Influence People* (Vermillion, 1994)

Mihaly Csikszentmihalyi, *Flow* (Rider, 2002)

Dalai Lama, *The Art of Happiness* (Riverhead Books, 1998)

Norman Doidge, *The Brain That Changes Itself* (Penguin, 2008)

Nikki Gemmel, Pleasure. *An Almanac For The Heart* (Fourth Estate, 2006)

Daniel Goleman, *Destructive Emotions and How We Can Overcome Them* (Bloomsbury, 2003)

Robert Emmons, *Thanks! How Practicing Gratitude Can Make You Happier* (Houghton Mifflin Harcourt, 2008)

Georgia Foster, *The Weight-Less Mind* (Foster Publishing, 2005)
------, *The Drink-Less Mind* (Foster Publishing, 2006)
------, *The 4 Secrets of Amazing Sex* (Georgia Foster Publising, 2008)
        www.georgiafoster.com – Hypnotherapy to change your life

Suzy Greaves, *Making The Big Leap* (New Holland, 2007)
    Suzy Greaves runs The Big Life Club:
                www.thebiglifeclub.com.
Join The Big Life Tribe – a membership site for those who want ongoing support on their Big Peace journey. Telephone 0845 430 0221 to contact the Big Leap offices.
    For career change, log on to: www.thebig-leap.com. For access to the free online 90-day Big Peace programme: www.thebigpeace.com

Seth Godin, *Tribes* (Piatkus, 2008)

Dr Edward M Hallowell, *Dare to Forgive* (Health Communications, 2006)

David Hamilton, *How Your Mind Can Heal Your Body* (Hay House, 2008)
    http://www.drdavidhamilton.com/ – Articles, information on cutting-edge brain science from my favourite doctor

Louise Hay, *You Can Heal Your Life* (Hay House, 1984)

Heartmath® – Get yourself an emWave Personal Stress Reliever machine (I call it my Big Peace machine). The emWave PSR reads your heart rhythms through a thumb or ear sensor and gives immediate feedback via changing colours and lights. By practising different Big Peace techniques, the machine gives you feedback on what works. www.heartmath.com

Carl Honoré, *In Praise of Slow* (Orion, 2005)

Byron Katie, *Loving What Is* (Rider, 2002)
    www.thework.com – Free workshops and regular updates on Byron Katie's work

Asara Lovejoy, *The One Command* (Wisdom House Books, 2007)

www.commandingwealth.com – For more information on The One Command process

Stephen and Ondrea Levine, *A Gradual Awakening* (Gateway, 1979)

James Maas, *Power Sleep* (HarperCollins, 1999)

Talane Miedaner, *Coach Yourself to Success* (McGraw-Hill, 2001)

Michael Neill, *Feel Happy Now!* (Hay House, 2007)

Dr Dean Ornish, *Dr. Dean Ornish's Program for Reversing Heart Disease* (Ballantine Books, 1992)

Dr James Pennebaker, *Opening Up* (Guilford, 1997)
------, *Writing to Heal* (New Harbinger Publications, 2004)

Dr Candace Pert, *Molecules of Emotion* (Pocket Books, 1999)

Matthieu Ricard, *Happiness, A Guide to Developing Life's Most Important Skill* (Atlantic Books, 2007)

Sogyal Rinpoche, *The Tibetan Book of Living and Dying* (Rider, 2002)

Don Richard Riso and Russ Hudson, *The Wisdom of the Enneagram* (Bantam, 1999)

Notes

Notes

Notes

Notes

Notes

Notes

Notes

Hay House Titles of Related Interest

The Art of Extreme Self-Care,
by Cheryl Richardson

Ask and It Is Given,
by Esther and Jerry Hicks

Everything I've Ever Done That Worked,
by Lesley Garner

How Your Mind Can Heal Your Body,
by David R. Hamilton PhD

Pure,
by Barefoot Doctor

The Shift DVD,
starring Wayne W. Dyer PhD

You Can Have What You Want,
by Michael Neill

We hope you enjoyed this Hay House book.
If you would like to receive a free catalogue featuring additional
Hay House books and products, or if you would like information
about the Hay Foundation, please contact:

Hay House UK Ltd
292B Kensal Road • London W10 5BE
Tel: (44) 20 8962 1230; Fax: (44) 20 8962 1239
www.hayhouse.co.uk

***

Published and distributed in the United States of America by:
Hay House, Inc. • PO Box 5100 • Carlsbad, CA 92018-5100
Tel: (1) 760 431 7695 or (1) 800 654 5126;
Fax: (1) 760 431 6948 or (1) 800 650 5115
www.hayhouse.com

***

Published and distributed in Australia by:
Hay House Australia Ltd • 18/36 Ralph Street • Alexandria, NSW 2015
Tel: (61) 2 9669 4299, Fax: (61) 2 9669 4144
www.hayhouse.com.au

***

Published and distributed in the Republic of South Africa by:
Hay House SA (Pty) Ltd • PO Box 990 • Witkoppen 2068
Tel/Fax: (27) 11 467 8904
www.hayhouse.co.za

***

Published and distributed in India by:
Hay House Publishers India • Muskaan Complex • Plot No.3
B-2• Vasant Kunj • New Delhi - 110 070
Tel: (91) 11 41761620; Fax: (91) 11 41761630
www.hayhouse.co.in

***

Distributed in Canada by:
Raincoast • 9050 Shaughnessy St • Vancouver, BC V6P 6E5
Tel: (1) 604 323 7100
Fax: (1) 604 323 2600

***

Sign up via the Hay House UK website to receive the Hay House
online newsletter and stay informed about what's going on with your
favourite authors. You'll receive bimonthly announcements
about discounts and offers, special events, product highlights,
free excerpts, giveaways, and more!
www.hayhouse.co.uk